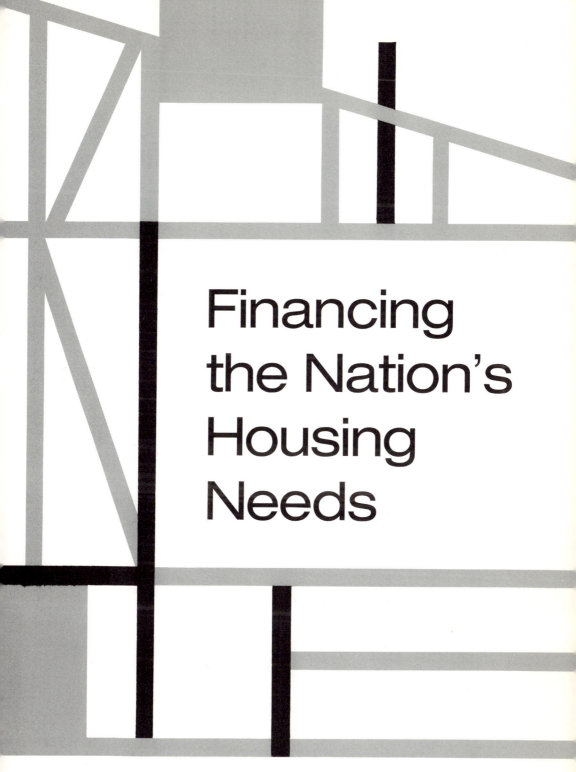

Financing
the Nation's
Housing
Needs

A Statement on National Policy
by the Research and Policy Committee
of the Committee for Economic Development
April, 1973 CED

Single copy . . . $1.50

Printed in U.S.A.
First Printing April 1973
Design: Harry Carter
Library of Congress Catalog Card Number: 73-77093
International Standard Book Number: 0-87186-050-3

73-4086
Committee for Economic Development
477 Madison Avenue, New York, N. Y. 10022

Contents

The Responsibility for
CED Statements on National Policy

This statement has been approved for publication as a statement of the Research and Policy Committee by the members of that Committee and its drafting subcommittee, subject to individual dissents or reservations noted herein. *The trustees who are responsible for this statement are listed on pages 5 and 6. Company associations are included for identification only; the companies do not share in the responsibility borne by the individuals.*

The Research and Policy Committee is directed by CED's bylaws to:

"Initiate studies into the principles of business policy and of public policy which will foster the full contribution by industry and commerce to the attainment and maintenance of high and secure standards of living for people in all walks of life through maximum employment and high productivity in the domestic economy."

The bylaws emphasize that:

"All research is to be thoroughly objective in character, and the approach in each instance is to be from the standpoint of the general welfare and not from that of any special political or economic group."

The Research and Policy Committee is composed of 60 Trustees from among the 200 businessmen and educators who comprise the Committee for Economic Development. It is aided by a Research Advisory Board of leading economists, a small permanent Research Staff, and by advisors chosen for their competence in the field being considered.

Each Statement on National Policy is preceded by discussions, meetings, and exchanges of memoranda, often stretching over many months. The research is undertaken by a subcommittee, with its advisors, and the full Research and Policy Committee participates in the drafting of findings and recommendations.

Except for the members of the Research and Policy Committee and the responsible subcommittee, the recommendations presented herein are not necessarily endorsed by other Trustees or by the advisors, contributors, staff members, or others associated with CED.

The Research and Policy Committee offers these Statements on National Policy as an aid to clearer understanding of the steps to be taken in achieving sustained growth of the American economy. The Committee is not attempting to pass on any pending specific legislative proposals; its purpose is to urge careful consideration of the objectives set forth in the statement and of the best means of accomplishing those objectives.

4.

Research and Policy Committee

Foreword

This policy statement reflects the Committee's awareness that it is impossible to isolate the nation's economic policy from its social needs. An area in which the social implications of economic policy decisions are especially significant is the housing sector. The reality is that housing production usually suffers when the rest of the economy flourishes. Since public policy has properly been directed at making high employment the norm, the effect of stabilization policies has on balance been to discriminate against housing activity.

In this report, we are especially concerned with the need to make the housing sector less vulnerable to cyclical fluctuations in the economy and to keep housing from being severely rationed in times of general prosperity. The Committee has recommended greater interest rate flexibility for mortgage lending institutions on both their loans and deposits, including the use of variable rate mortgages. At the same time, we have pointed out that the single most important means of avoiding cyclical disruption lies in the pursuit of sound fiscal policies. This would eliminate the need to rely on excessively tight monetary policies, which sharply limit the flow of funds to housing.

Although we have concentrated on economic and financial policies to improve the functioning of private markets, we were also concerned with the need to improve the housing condition of that part of the nation that still lives in housing poverty.

This policy statement was prepared and approved for publication before the Administration announced a freeze on subsidies for the construction of new housing for low- and moderate-income families. The Committee therefore has not commented explicitly on this important development in national housing policy. But it is apparent that if the expenditure budget is to be lowered, there must be cutbacks in some programs.

We share the Administration's concern with the inefficiencies in the execution of present housing programs, which are based on credit subsidies for housing construction and which have resulted in high cost and varied inequities. Indeed, we recommend in this report consideration of a large-scale, national program providing housing allowances directly to low-income families as a substitute for the credit subsidy approach, after adequate testing of its feasibility.

Nevertheless, the Committee believes that because of the great housing need that remains unfilled, the credit subsidy programs should not be phased out until they are replaced by a sound alternative. In the Committee's view, subsidies provided for the building of new houses must be continued, with administrative and other deficiencies vigorously corrected.

The moratorium on housing subsidies must be evaluated in the context of the growing demand for housing which has resulted from the rise in population and the continued loss of existing stock through deterioration and abandonment. This policy is therefore inconsistent with the commitment that the nation made over two decades ago to assure "as soon as feasible . . . a decent home and suitable living environment for every American family." This goal, set forth in the Housing Act of 1949, was affirmed by Congress as recently as 1968, when Congress declared it "a matter of grave national concern" that the goal of adequate housing for all has not been fully realized for many of the nation's lower-income families.

The Research and Policy Committee extends its thanks to all the members of the subcommittee and the many advisors who participated in this project. We appreciate as well the research and drafting contributions of Robert Lindsay, Project Director; Frank W. Schiff, Associate Project Director; and Jacob Worenklein, CED's Associate Director of Information.

Philip M. Klutznick, *Chairman*
Marvin Bower, *Co-Chairman*
Research and Policy Committee

8.

Chapter 1

· · · · · · · · · · · · ·

Introduction and Summary

The housing condition of the American people has improved enormously since the 1930s, when one third of the nation was considered "ill housed" even by Depression standards. Yet one out of every seven households in the nation still lives in "housing poverty," as measured by the much higher standards of today. At the same time, many families with adequate housing must spend such a large portion of their income for shelter that they are forced to scrimp on the necessities of food, clothing, and other basic items.

The problems of housing finance, however, affect far more people than the small minority of the housing poor. It cannot lightly be assumed, for example, that the necessary supply of housing will automatically be forthcoming even for middle-class families with incomes well above the poverty level. In one way or another, problems of housing finance affect everyone.

Housing policy, therefore, must assure the availability of sufficient housing to fill the needs of all sectors of society during the 1970s—through efficiently functioning private markets for the vast majority of Americans and through government subsidies for the housing poor. Although this policy statement on housing finance must by nature be technical, it is important not to lose sight of the fundamental human issues with which we are concerned.*

The subject of housing finance also involves basic issues of economic policy. It is impossible to overemphasize, for example, the degree to which housing affects—and is in turn affected by—fiscal and monetary stabilization policy. One of the purposes of this statement, therefore, is to assure that economic and housing measures are properly coordinated.

It is now over two decades since the nation dedicated itself to the goal of assuring a "decent home and a suitable living environment for every American family." Toward this end the federal government launched a variety of programs to create housing directly and to establish favorable conditions for private housing construction. A large volume of new housing has been brought into being, the quality of the housing stock has been raised far higher than ever before, and the large potential risks of homebuilding and home-owning have been greatly reduced.

Yet despite these long-term successes, the programs currently in force seem to be in deep trouble. They have created widespread public uneasiness and a rising volume of criticism about their adequacy, fairness, and efficiency.

The tools designed to produce housing outside the normal reach of the private housing market have proved especially disappointing. The construction of new, subsidized living quarters for lower-income families has fallen far behind the schedule adopted for achieving the ten-year goals proclaimed by Congress in the Housing and Urban Development Act of 1968. At the same time, the supply of low-cost housing already in existence has been reduced by the rapid deterioration of many inner-city neighborhoods** and the abrupt abandonment of older but otherwise sound housing structures. The costs of subsidy programs have also risen sharply, and more recently the programs have been further discredited by the evidence of corruption in their administration in a number of cities.

---

*See Memorandum by MR. R. STEWART RAUCH, JR., page 56.
**See Memorandum by MR. H. C. TURNER, JR., page 56.

In the private housing market, performance in the last several years has exceeded the targets established by Congress in 1968. Yet even in the private market, a sharp tightening in the credit and money markets would put the system under considerable strain. Significant interruptions in the housing supply are a distinct possibility.

This statement examines the financial obstacles that hinder fulfillment of the nation's housing requirements—both in the part of the market that is directly subsidized and in the much larger part that is unsubsidized. The recommendations set forth below are aimed at making the nation's housing markets more responsive to the needs of all sectors of our society.*

Housing policy in the United States must resolve three major financial problems: (1) It must provide the total amount of financing required to meet the nation's housing needs in the 1970s. (2) It must minimize the cyclical disruptions in housing finance that stem from fluctuations in business activity and that tend to be magnified by the especially severe impact of monetary policy on the housing sector. (3) It must aid those whose incomes are insufficient to pay for housing of minimum standards —the housing poor who constitute more than one in every seven households.

There are, of course, many other important issues of housing policy, but they are not directly financial in nature. For the reasons set forth at the end of this chapter, we have concentrated our attention on the three issues listed above.

Financing Requirements for the 1970s

The housing sector has long faced special difficulties in attracting adequate financing. Individual families and most building firms—the ultimate borrowers of mortgage credit—are too small to have direct access to capital markets. Yet the inherent characteristics of residential finance have made it very difficult for households and small builders to market mortgages directly on a substantial scale. For housing loans are necessarily large, relative to the annual income of these borrowers, and long-term, relative to their income-earning years. Thus, to protect themselves against risk, lenders must examine directly each individual house and lot

---

*See Memorandum by MR. OSCAR A. LUNDIN, page 56.

that serves as collateral for such loans. Each mortgage must be custom-built.

These characteristics have led to the development of highly specialized lending operations. Mortgage lending is the principal activity of savings and loan associations and mutual savings banks, and these "thrift institutions" account for about 60 per cent of all residential mortgage lending. Mortgage operations are also carried out in separate departments of broad-gauged lending institutions, such as commercial banks and insurance companies, which together account for less than 30 per cent of residential mortgages.

Specialization in mortgage loans, however, has exposed lenders to a number of difficulties. The interest rates they may charge on mortgage loans are subject to ceilings which have often proved inflexible. In addition, the thrift institutions have traditionally depended on short-term savings deposits as a source of funds to be loaned to mortgage borrowers. However, in the late 1950s, these institutions started facing much sharper competition. Funds that previously had flowed into the thrift institutions, and through them into the mortgage markets, were directed more and more into commercial banks and into the open market. As a consequence, a larger share of such funds went into other, nonmortgage types of lending.

In the late 1960s it became increasingly evident that the existing financing structure was failing to supply the volume of housing finance the nation seemed to need. At the same time, there was a growing realization that the postwar baby boom would soon begin to produce a further major demand for housing, thus requiring in the 1970s a very considerable expansion in the nation's stock of high quality, usable housing.

Congress, in recognition of these special pressures, set explicit housing goals for the nation. The Housing and Urban Development Act of 1968 pledged federal aid in building or rehabilitating 26 million housing units over the next decade. In addition, the federal government launched a number of new financing programs to assist in the achievement of these goals. The flurry of legislative and administrative innovations created a new system for linking mortgage borrowers with the securities markets. In effect, mortgage loans were transformed into instruments tradeable in the securities markets, attracting new sources of finance for housing.

These breakthroughs have spurred further innovations. Banks and other lenders have broken away from older patterns, entering new loan markets and seeking out new sources of funds. New instruments have been created by private firms for tapping the capital markets in large volume, paralleling the practice of federal agencies that issue their own debentures and then channel the proceeds into residential mortgage markets. Private insurance of mortgage credit has grown to rival federal insurance. Indeed, so major were the breakthroughs in the late 1960s that the process of adaptation and change will undoubtedly continue well into the 1970s.

All these advances in financial technology, however, cannot simply be added together. Some cancel each other out. Thus, one of the important issues in housing policy for the decade of the seventies is whether all these devices together will be sufficient to finance the necessary expansion of the housing stock without distortion and high cost.

Moreover, a number of serious problems persist despite the great advances, and may work to unduly dampen the flow of funds into housing during the 1970s. For example, constraints on mortgage interest rates as a result of usury laws and other rate ceilings have continued to redirect credit away from mortgages and into other competing uses. One consequence is that life insurance companies, once a major source, have begun in recent years to put a major share of their construction funds into nonresidential uses, with less and less available for residential financing, particularly for single-family homes.

With so much evolution in the financial structure still under way, it is difficult to project the total volume of mortgage funds that the emerging system will be capable of producing as the decade proceeds. In this dynamic atmosphere, we think that the prevailing spirit must be a willingness to experiment with new forms and new techniques. In such a changing time, more than ever before, it is essential to market-test new ideas before accepting or rejecting them. This does not mean, however, suspending all existing programs, which have succeeded in providing a substantial volume of needed housing, while we search for better alternatives.

We believe that the total flow of funds required during this decade can be met with the level of federal subsidy support envisioned in the Housing and Urban Development Act of 1968 and with the present and evolving assortment of financial mechanisms—but only if there is neither a general capital shortage nor serious cyclical disruption.

The danger of a general capital shortage, however, is a real one because of the inability of the present federal tax system in recent years of inflation to generate revenues on a high-employment basis equal to the committed levels of government spending—and the frequent unwillingness of the public and their elected officials to pay for the services they demand.

Determined action by both the Congress and the Executive Branch is required to assure that the federal budget will at least be in balance at a high level of employment or in moderate surplus when the economy is operating at high employment under inflationary pressures. If this condition is not met and persistent federal deficits and excessively heavy federal borrowings in the capital market contribute to a general capital shortage, the availability of funds for the mortgage market and the housing sector will be significantly curtailed. The task of avoiding large-scale budget deficits in the mid-1970s will not be easy. **We urge, therefore, that the President and the Congress give the highest priority in 1973 to the implementation of fiscal plans and procedures that will permit achievement of a budget surplus or at least balance when high employment is reached.**[1] We underscore our strong belief that sound fiscal policy is an absolute prerequisite not only to the provision of adequate levels of housing but to the solution of many of the most serious problems confronting the nation.

Cyclical Disruption

The story of housing construction over the years has been an erratic story of sharp spurts and slumps, which have been a key source of the greatly increased cost of housing in recent years. If repeated episodes of cyclical disruption occur in the 1970s, the total housing needs of the decade cannot possibly be met. In addition, each episode of cyclical disruption, each interruption, creates immediate economic and social costs.

For cyclical disruption is not a mere technical issue. It affects major elements of people's lives. It creates turmoil for the housing industry, for consumers of housing, and for the entire financial system in which all borrowers and savers, large and small, have an important stake. Moreover, it makes more difficult the containment of inflation,

---

1/For more detailed recommendations, see *High Employment Without Inflation: A Positive Program for Economic Stabilization,* A Statement on National Policy by the Research and Policy Committee, Committee for Economic Development (July 1972), pp. 31-34.

as the instability and irregularity of work undermines productivity, increases pressure for excessive compensation, and reinforces discriminations that create bottlenecks in supply. The importance of achieving *stable* levels of production can therefore not be emphasized enough.

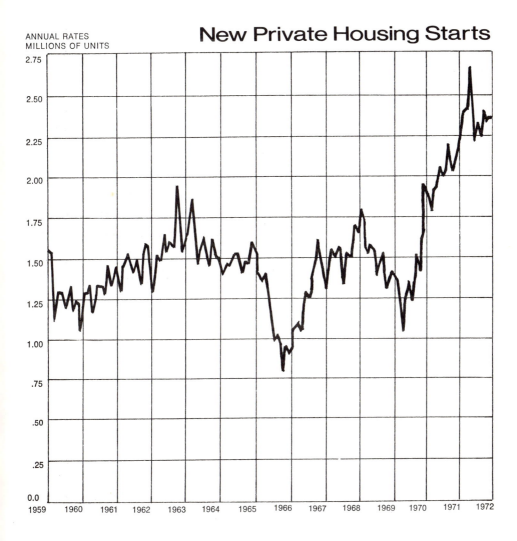

ANNUAL RATES
MILLIONS OF UNITS

New Private Housing Starts

The housing sector is unusually vulnerable to cyclical fluctuations. The ultimate borrowers of mortgage credit—the households—appear to be more sensitive to interest rate increases than business borrowers. Thus with rising interest rates, demand falls. But in addition, some major suppliers of mortgage funds—the thrift institutions—are highly sensitive to tightening monetary conditions. In essence, these institutions *intermediate* between small savers who want a highly liquid earning asset, and investors who want to borrow for long periods. In the middle and late

15.

1960s, however, as an excessive reliance on monetary policy pushed interest rates sharply upward in the securities and short-term money markets, many depositors pulled their funds out of the thrift institutions. They invested the funds directly in the markets instead of having the intermediaries do it for them. Where before there had been *intermediation,* the thrift institutions were suddenly faced with *disintermediation.* Enormous pressures resulted in all sectors of the banking system. The pressures on the mutual savings banks and savings and loan associations, however, were most severe. With the credit crunch on, the level of new construction fell sharply.

Conversely, when credit conditions ease, a sharp increase in deposit flows to these institutions can create wide fluctuations in the opposite direction. Indeed, there is a very real danger that the system now being developed for increasing the total flow of residential mortgage money is at the same time enlarging the risk of excessive fluctuations in the flow of mortgage credit. The federal intermediaries,[2] which channel funds from the securities market to mortgage borrowers, have become a much larger source of mortgage flows, but to some extent at the wrong time of the cycle. By some of their actions, they encourage—rather than dampen—the countercyclical character of housing and housing finance. For example, in the second half of 1971, when new savings were flooding into the thrift institutions in unprecedented volume, the net injection of mortgage money by federally-sponsored credit agencies rose to an annual rate of $8 billion—also an unprecedented level. Moreover, when the cycle turns, the overuse of their intermediation ability may be succeeded by an underuse of these powers when most needed. Even a return to a normal level would mean a reduction of the flow of mortgage money.

A further danger would arise, moreover, if federal agency efforts to tap the capital markets are pursued too vigorously. While these efforts may on balance add to the total flow of mortgage credit, they may in the process also push interest rates significantly higher. If they do, deposits would be drained away from the private financial intermediaries, as now constituted, badly crimping their lending power and even threatening their viability.

2/The four major institutions are the Federal Home Loan Bank System (FHLBS), Federal Home Loan Mortgage Corporation (FHLMC), the Federal National Mortgage Association (FNMA), and the Government National Mortgage Association (GNMA). In addition, there are the Federal Housing Authority (FHA) and the Veterans Administration (VA), which provide insurance or guarantees for mortgages which meet certain conditions.

The following set of recommendations, therefore, is designed to assure an adequate level of housing finance by reducing cyclical disruption.

The single most important means of avoiding such disruption lies in the pursuit of sound fiscal policies. This would eliminate the need to rely on excessively tight monetary policies, which sharply restrict the flow of funds for housing.

To keep mortgage lending institutions viable, it is also essential that they be allowed greater interest rate flexibility. It is crucial that when market interest rates begin to rise, these institutions not be locked into relatively low interest rates on either their loans or their deposits. For if they cannot adjust their rates to meet market conditions, they will be able neither to attract the necessary deposits from savers nor to charge borrowers enough to make mortgage loans competitive with other potential uses of the banks' funds.

We urge that the federal government endorse and publicize its support of private experiments with variable rate mortgages as a standard mode of doing business. We applaud the proposals of the Federal Home Loan Bank Board supporting variable rate mortgages. We recommend that similar action be taken deliberately and systematically by all agencies that buy and sell mortgages or provide direct or indirect subsidies. Indeed, we recommend that the federal agencies seek ways to reward private experimentation in writing variable rate contracts. Precautions must be taken, however, to ensure that borrowers are protected and not exploited.

The purpose of the variable rate mortgage is to enable the thrift institutions to stay liquid and flexible and to serve the needs of the public. It is not a vehicle for enriching institutions, and the borrowers must share in the benefits when interest rates fall.

We expect that borrowers will be offered lower initial rates than those being quoted on fixed rate mortgages if they will agree to have rates move up and down with some stated index. **We recommend in particular the "variable maturity" instrument—a mortgage contract in which the rate is changed by lengthening or shortening the maturity of the mortgage, not by raising or lowering the monthly payment to be made by the mortgager.** When interest rates are rising, this will allow the lending institutions to treat a larger part of their monthly payment receipts as return on capital.

As a second major step toward the interest rate flexibility necessary to keep thrift institutions viable as mortgage lenders, we urge greater

flexibility of interest rate ceilings on mortgages and on savings accounts, allowing them to vary with changing market conditions. The sole purpose of such ceilings should be to set outer boundaries for safety. The ceilings, however, should interfere as little as possible with natural market forces.

As an interim step toward lifting interest rate ceilings entirely and holding them in a standby status, the FHA and VA should be permitted to adopt the dual rate system proposed by the Commission on Mortgage Interest Rates. Lenders and borrowers would then have the choice of (a) using the present arrangement in which the lender can charge no more than a specified number of discount points to supplement the stated ceiling or (b) freely negotiating the interest rate to be charged, with no discounts permitted.

In time, such ceilings should be lifted completely if experience with the full assortment of new financial tools and instruments warrants such a change. Even then, however, standby authority should be maintained to reimpose interest rate ceilings if necessary.

State usury ceilings, too, have presented serious problems. Where it does not seem feasible to remove these ceilings entirely, we urge that they be raised well above the average mortgage rates of recent years.

Implementation of this set of recommendations should help assure the continued, long-term viability of the $350 billion "thrift institutions"—the savings and loan associations and mutual savings banks—which are by far the most important source of mortgage lending today. We recognize, however, that these recommendations will not provide a rapid solution to the problem of cyclical disruption since it will take time before variable rate mortgages become a significant part of loan portfolios, and even then such mortgages might be spread unevenly among the thrift institutions.

A potentially powerful source of protection against cyclical disruption are the federal intermediaries. However, because the federal intermediaries are independent or quasi-independent institutions, we are concerned that they may not do enough to dampen the wide cyclical swings which afflict the housing sector. The Federal National Mortgage Association (FNMA) presents a particular problem as a privately-owned entity with a major public responsibility.

We urge that a clear set of guidelines be developed for the federal intermediaries, setting out as precisely as possible their roles and responsibilities as part of a coherent national housing policy.

The federal intermediaries, of course, do not operate in a policy vacuum. Their activities are affected to a major degree by the actions of other government agencies. From time to time, these actions conflict with each other—sometimes inevitably, sometimes unnecessarily.

To develop and coordinate the implementation of internally consistent policies, a formal mechanism is needed that will draw all the federal and quasi-federal housing agencies into the monetary and fiscal policy decision-making process of the federal government. We recommend that the informal committees of recent administrations be succeeded by a formal, systematic council within the Executive Branch.

Toward this same end, we repeat our earlier endorsement of the proposed Federal Financing Bank to coordinate federal agency borrowing and guarantee programs.[3] We recommend, as we did in our previous statement, that the President be authorized to place limits on the total volume of loan guarantees and of borrowing by federal and federally sponsored credit agencies, including those that are privately owned.

It is especially important that housing not be made the principal vehicle of general monetary policy restraint. The guidelines should assure that credit restrictions do not fall unduly on any one sector. When monetary policy decisions are made, the cyclical problems of housing should receive special attention because of their great severity.

We also recommend that the guidelines to federal agencies make clear and mandatory the responsibility of the federal housing intermediaries for concentrating their assistance in periods when the private institutions are experiencing most difficulty in attracting savings deposits.

We urge the enactment of legislation mandating the federal and quasi-federal housing intermediaries to act to counter the cycle in housing activity and to narrow its amplitude, not to encourage wider swings up or down.

These recommendations are not aimed at shifting the pattern of the housing cycle to make it coincide with fluctuations in the general economy, but rather are designed to smooth down the amplitude of the housing cycle. Our recommendations would have a twofold effect. First, they would make it easier for thrift institutions to ride out the storm of fluctuations in interest rates. And, second, they would clearly orient federal intermediation to work chiefly as a counterforce to private disintermediation.

3/*High Employment Without Inflation: A Positive Program for Economic Stabilization,* A Statement on National Policy by the Research and Policy Committee, Committee for Economic Development (July 1972).

The Problem of Housing Poverty

An extremely pressing problem of housing finance is the inadequacy of housing available to the poorer sectors of society, the problem of housing poverty. The prevailing approach to this problem has been to provide subsidies in the form of credit to be used in building, acquiring, and managing housing for the poor. This method, however, does not get at the root of the problem. Providing cheap credit is not an adequate response to housing poverty. Even at a zero rate of interest, there are many households whose incomes are insufficient to pay for housing of minimum standards. Moreover, such an approach, focusing heavily on the construction of new housing, does not sufficiently aid the owners and tenants of used housing, although they are vast in number and although subsidizing used housing is often cheaper than new construction.

In recent years, furthermore, the credit subsidy programs have provided more extensive benefits for people above the poverty line than for those below. As Appendix A to this statement points out, the benefits of housing subsidies have been concentrated in the upper-income levels.

A housing policy which favors families above the poverty line and emphasizes the need for new construction must implicitly assume that low-income families will be assisted indirectly. The assumption is that through the efficient working of the "filtering" process, newly built homes will release older ones, which can then filter down to levels the poor can afford. Thus, instead of raising the incomes of the poor so that they can rent or purchase adequate housing, the filtering policy assumes that rents and prices of older houses will fall to within the reach of the poor. Such an approach leaves the way open, obviously, to very low standards of housing for the poor, which even then may take a large share of their low incomes.

The excessive costs, inefficiencies, and inequities of subsidy programs as well as the inadequacies in the filtering strategy which the United States has pursued lead us to recommend a change in direction for the nation's housing policy.

We urge a major shift in the allocation of subsidies for low-income families. A much greater share of the public subsidies for housing must be channeled to those at the bottom of the income ladder.

We strongly support a large-scale, national program providing housing allowances directly to low-income families. * Such a program

*See Memorandum by MR. E. SHERMAN ADAMS, page 57.

would provide eligible households with the means to pay for the cost of adequate housing. Households would be required to pay a specified percentage—about one-fourth—of income for rent. The housing allowance in turn would provide the difference between this sum and the shelter costs for units which meet a minimum specified level of adequacy.

The cost of such a housing allowance program at the present level of assistance to the housing poor need not be any greater than subsidies in their present form and may well be less. Of course, extension of housing allowances to all families who might be deemed eligible under present standards (such as the households who are now on waiting lists for public housing) would add significantly to the cost of a housing allowance program, just as the direct provision of housing to such families would greatly increase the cost of present programs.[4] Under current economic and budgetary conditions, however, the housing allowance program must be designed and implemented so that a significant inflationary impact is avoided and excessive pressure is not placed on the federal budget.*

Because much remains to be learned about the impact and the most effective means of mounting and administering housing allowance programs, we endorse the systematic experimentation already begun by federal agencies. These experiments are needed *not* for deciding whether the country should have such programs, but rather for determining how best to design them.

For the foreseeable future, we recommend that income supplements be tied directly to housing, including used as well as new housing. Ultimately, these income supplements should be incorporated into the more general programs of income maintenance, with the recipients free to allocate the funds according to their own priorities.[5] Even within this freedom of choice, the size of payments might be varied in different parts of the country to take account of regional differentials in housing costs. Ideally and ultimately, the level of income supplements would be high enough everywhere to permit the recipients flexibility in allocating the funds, but this would seem to lie still further in the future.

4/Recent studies for The Brookings Institution and the Urban Institute have estimated that a full-scale housing allowance program covering a larger portion of the housing poor than the present program will cost between $3.2 and $7 billion annually, depending on the scope of coverage and the subsidy's impact on housing costs. The net cost, of course, will be smaller as the housing allowance program replaces existing programs.

5/*Improving the Public Welfare System,* A Statement on National Policy by the Research and Policy Committee, Committee for Economic Development (April 1970).

*See Memorandum by MR. DAVIDSON SOMMERS, page 57.

Until housing allowances are a reality on a large scale, subsidies provided through the building of new houses should be continued. They should not be cut back while the housing allowance experiments are taking place. If the pace of new construction is not increased or at least maintained at current levels, the growth in the housing stock will fall significantly behind the need. For one thing, the population continues to grow and move. Moreover, until we can learn how to stem the large-scale abandonment of physically sound housing in many central cities, the high levels of abandonment will require still further growth in the housing stock.*

Once an effective design of housing allowances has been selected, the construction subsidies can be phased down as the housing allowance program takes effect. However, even after the housing allowance program is fully established, some minimal subsidies to new construction may continue to be necessary.*

We are, of course, aware of the recent rash of scandals in some of the programs for subsidizing construction for middle- and low-income families. These do not, however, seem to us a reason for abandoning all such efforts. What is called for is a reconsideration of the conceptual design of some of the newer programs and, even more urgently, improved administration of all the credit subsidy programs along lines already identified by the Department of Housing and Urban Development in its own audits.

We also emphasize the importance of providing greater amenities in low-income housing programs. In addition, we urge a greater effort to increase supply by drawing used housing into the stock that is made available to low-income families.

Whatever the form, housing assistance for low-income families should not be confined to the older, more urban areas. While urban life has vibrance and excitement and special cultural advantages, the suburbs offer major advantages of their own. The important need is a greater range of choice for low-income families, including, if they want it, access to areas of lower density. In some localities this will require subsidies for the construction of new housing.*

In sum, because the markets work so badly for the poor, financial assistance must be provided for both supply and demand. It must, at the same time, produce more housing units and make possible more consumption of housing services.

---

*See Memoranda by MR. ROBERT C. WEAVER, pages 57 and 58.

22.

Scope of the Statement

In addition to the questions addressed above we recognize that there is a very pressing set of policy issues stemming from needs beyond shelter. They include education, transportation, garbage collection, crime and fire protection, and all the other essential features of community life that supplement the physical structure of a dwelling place. We also recognize that even the shelter needs may not be fully met if new housing is not accompanied by new infrastructures—the waterworks, sewage, and roadways necessary to make the building accessible and inhabitable. In addition, there are the sometimes arbitrary building codes and other legal and social barriers which reduce the availability and increase the cost of housing in many areas.

This statement will not try to deal with these financial problems, important as they are, and as closely allied as they are to housing finance.[6] They are, to begin with, enormously complex, and far beyond the scope of a single statement of this kind. Furthermore, their financial content is largely *public* finance, centering around the proper funding of state and local governments and the sharing of revenues between different levels of government. Finally, and most important, these issues sprawl well beyond finance of any kind. They go deep toward the center of major debates about the social contract of our times—racial integration, the fragmentation of political organization in metropolitan areas, the design of cities, the functioning of the economy itself.

Accordingly, because we believe that the availability of adequate financing is itself a fundamental step to the solution of the nation's housing problems, we concentrate our attention here on three issues directly related to housing finance: the total financing needs of the 1970s, the profound cyclical disturbances that housing suffers, and the special problems stemming from the unequal distribution of income among the occupants of housing.

6/The CED Research and Policy Committee has issued statements on national policy dealing with a number of these problems, including welfare reform, education, training and job programs, crime, health care, and the organization of local and metropolitan government.

Chapter 2

· · · · · · · · · · · · ·

Financing
the Nation's Housing
Markets

The extensive network of public and private agencies of housing finance developed over the last decade is somewhat more likely to succeed in supplying the total requirements of housing finance in the 1970s than it is in reducing the disruptive impact of interest rate fluctuations. Since interest rate stability over the 1970s is unlikely, the cyclical problem of housing requires a continued search for solutions. Moreover, there is a need to restructure the process of private mortgage lending in order to maintain its health in the face of wide swings in interest rates. Failure to do so would cause further inflation of housing costs and would endanger the ability of the system to deliver the full volume of housing finance needed in the aggregate over the decade. The two problems are tied together.

The Size and Shape
of Housing Finance in the 1970s

The number of new housing units that the country will need to build during the 1970s cannot be known, of course, with any precision. A general order of magnitude, however, is both possible and useful.

Some surge in demand is certain to come from population growth, with a sharp rise in new family formation inescapable. The nation's birth rate burst upward at the end of World War II, rose further in the 1950s and remained above prewar levels until the middle 1960s. Thus, the number of people entering the age brackets from which new households are formed will be large for some time to come.

Partly in anticipation of this growth, the Housing and Urban Development Act of 1968 established for the first time a numerical goal for the nation's housing. The target for the decade ending in 1978, as slightly modified since initial passage of the Act, is 26 million new and rehabilitated units. Of this total, 20 million would provide for the new demand from population growth and for the normal replacement of existing houses of standard quality. The remaining 6 million would be subsidized in order to upgrade the housing of low-income families by replacing substandard dwellings with new or rehabilitated houses.

In the meantime, a further longer-term pressure for housing finance has been created by the rise of the abandonment phenomenon —the premature loss from the housing stock of structurally sound dwellings. In part, abandonment is itself a consequence of too little finance. Hence, the total funds needed in the 1970s will require an increased flow of money, either to prevent early abandonment or to provide extra new houses to offset the dwelling units that leave the usable housing stock in this fashion.

A final element which must be included in any assessment of demand is the rate of vacancies to be maintained in the usable stock.

Despite uncertainties over the level of demand, two separate studies have resulted in similar projections for the overall level of housing starts.[1] The projections indicate that the demand for housing will approach an average of 2,500,000 units a year—the goal set forth in the

---

1/Sherman Maisel, "Money and Housing," speech to Producers' Council Conference, Washington, D.C., May 6, 1971; and Charles L. Schultze et al., *Setting National Priorities: The 1972 Budget* (Washington, D.C.: The Brookings Institution, 1971), pp. 282-288.

Housing and Urban Development Act of 1968—and that the needed supply will be forthcoming without great strain.

Fewer efforts have been made to quantify the general capacity of the financial system to provide the necessary funds for these goals. The system is complicated, with many interconnections and a considerable degree of fluidity. As a result, long-range projections require a number of detailed and interlocking subsidiary projections and many specific assumptions, any one of which may go wide of the mark. One excellent example of such an effort is available from the recent Housing Study by the staff of the Board of Governors of the Federal Reserve System.[2] This particular example illustrates the large amount of residual ambiguity in such projections, but also indicates the general orders of magnitude that the financial system can reasonably be expected to achieve.

The analysis contains three important conclusions concerning the general availability of housing finance over the balance of this decade:

1. The financing necessary to meet the housing goals of 1970 will not strain either the real economy or its financial capacity, under the conditions assumed. By 1980, net new borrowing in the form of housing mortgages would represent a larger percentage of GNP than in the last half of the 1960s, and also a larger portion of total funds borrowed than in those years. By either measure, however, the pressure would be no greater than it was in the first half of the 1960s or the last half of the 1950s. (See Appendix Table B-1, lines A-6 and B-6.)

2. For these funds to be forthcoming, federally sponsored agencies such as FNMA would continue to be needed as supplements to lending by private intermediaries. This support, stated as a per cent of GNP, would have to exceed significantly the levels of the late 1950s and particularly those of the early 1960s, but it would not have to remain high as in the late 1960s. (See Appendix Table B-2, line A-5.)

3. Assuming the federal budget to be approximately in balance, the public securities markets would be in good position to absorb the federal agency debt issues necessary to raise funds for their mortgage support operations.

2/Stephen P. Taylor, "Long-Term Prospects for Housing Finance—A Projection to 1980," *Federal Reserve Staff Study: Ways to Moderate Fluctuations in Housing Construction* (Washington, D.C.: Board of Governors of the Federal Reserve System, December 1972).

Thus, on the assumptions given and taking no account of short-run cyclical disruptions, the present structure of financial instruments and institutions would appear to be capable of producing the funds necessary for the housing activity prescribed in the national goals for the 1970s.

As already noted, however, actual trends in the budget during recent years have thrown a deep shadow over one of the critical assumptions of the Federal Reserve projections — the assumption that under conditions of high employment the federal budget would be close to balance through much of the decade. **We urge, therefore, that the President and the Congress give the highest priority in 1973 to the implementation of fiscal plans and procedures that will permit achievement of a budget surplus or at least balance when high employment is reached.**[3] We underscore our strong belief that sound fiscal policy is an absolute prerequisite not only to the provision of adequate levels of housing but to the solution of the many other serious problems confronting the nation.

Unless the necessary fiscal policy actions are taken, the capital markets are likely to experience frequent periods of extremely severe pressure under these circumstances. If further innovation does not occur in private intermediation, support from the federally sponsored agencies will have to approach or exceed the high levels reached in the late 1960s. It may prove difficult to achieve the national housing goals without some reordering of other national priorities.

The longer-term projections discussed here also assume that a high employment surplus in the federal budget will not be achieved at the expense of the federal subsidy programs for low- and middle-income housing. Indeed, any failure to achieve the subsidy levels envisioned in the Housing and Urban Development Act of 1968, and particularly any significant interruption in the flow of these funds, will make it very difficult to produce the total volume of housing finance required over the decade.

Still another source of possible difficulty is the flow of *equity* financing to housing, particularly large-scale apartment housing. The purchase of single-family dwellings has become less dependent on equity funds than before, as lenders and private mortgage insurance firms experiment with "piggyback" second mortgages and other innovations. But while creativity has also been at work in multifamily financing, the tax

---

3/For more detailed recommendations, see *High Employment Without Inflation: A Positive Program for Economic Stabilization*, A Statement on National Policy by the Research and Policy Committee, Committee for Economic Development (July 1972), pp. 31-34.

laws have served as a major stimulus. With multifamily housing expected to account for a rising share of all new residential construction over the 1970s, a shortage of equity funds in that sector as a result of tax changes could prove especially troublesome.

The Vulnerability to Wide Swings in Interest Rates

Whether or not the total need can be met without severe strain, there is almost certainly a continuing danger of cyclical disruption. This problem has two major parts to it. One is the continued exposure of the thrift institutions to disintermediation—withdrawal of funds by depositors in order to invest them directly in open market securities when short-term interest rates rise. The other part of the cyclical disruption problem involves deficiencies in the design and behavior of the federal intermediaries created in recent years to stabilize the flow of mortgage money.

The Spectre of Private Disintermediation

The impact of the economy on housing is a matter of special concern because the swings in housing activity are so much wider than fluctuations in the rest of the economy. For workers and firms in the housing business and for consumers of housing services, these swings impose a burden far beyond the norm in our society.

If large numbers of workers are left idle when housing activity goes slack, they have less chance of being readily absorbed into other employment. Moreover, if and when they do eventually find other positions, the next sharp upswing in residential construction will again require a large reshuffling back in the other direction. This shift, furthermore, will be all the more clumsy if skills have grown rusty in the meantime or if large numbers of new people with little or no skills will have to be recruited and trained.

All of this is bound to put upward pressure on the cost of housing services. To be sure, layoff and recall is a common sequence in American industry. The wider the swings and the more massive the transfers, however, the more potential there is for hardship and for extra cost in matching together the large numbers of workers with large expansions in new jobs.

A further reason for concern stems from the fact that the housing sector tends to be strong when the economy as a whole is weak and to do poorly when most of the rest of the economy flourishes. Over longer periods, this would not necessarily result in an undue dampening of housing activity if periods of general prosperity and general slack were to be of about equal duration. But since public policy has properly been directed at making high employment the norm, the effect of stabilization policies has on balance been to discriminate against housing activity. Some way must be found to keep this sector from being so severely rationed in times of general prosperity.

Both the extraordinary amplitude of fluctuations and the counter-cyclical pattern of housing activity appear to be profoundly financial in nature. To begin with, new construction and the purchase and sale of existing houses are sensitive to the cost of mortgage credit, which quickly rises with general recovery. A second influence is that commercial banks, although major suppliers of mortgage credit, tend to specialize most heavily in business loans and thus feel a primary allegiance to business borrowers. As corporate needs for credit begin to revive, these lenders turn away from mortgage lending. Many potential mortgage borrowers find that credit is simply unavailable. For such lenders, housing finance is a residual claimant, a market to be supplied when other demands are at their lowest ebb, but one to be set aside when the nonhousing tide comes in again.

A third and very large reason for the great fluctuations in housing finance and for its countercyclical character is that some major mortgage lenders are themselves the victims of the cyclical process. When non-housing demands for credit rise, they too are set aside along with mortgage borrowers. When general recovery hits the credit markets, these institutions suffer *disintermediation*. Normally, these lending institutions —savings and loan associations and mutual savings banks in particular— provide *intermediation*. That is, they serve as go-betweens connecting savers who want a highly liquid asset with investors who want to borrow for long periods. They meet the needs of savers and investors who could not very well do business directly with one another. They assemble small packets of short-term money and relend it in larger bundles with longer maturity. In a word, they intermediate.

In 1966, and again at the end of the decade, this process of inter-mediation was reversed and disintermediation resulted. Interest rates on other kinds of assets rose so rapidly that owners of savings accounts at financial intermediaries were tempted into these open markets on a much larger scale than ever before. If financial institutions had been able to follow the market closely and raise the rates they were paying for savings accounts, they might have fought off this competition. But they felt unable to compete adequately because their earning assets—which were long-lived and acquired at much lower rates—did not yield enough to justify competitive increases in the interest rates they were offering on savings accounts. Official ceilings on these interest rates were a further constraint.

Thus, the fortunes of one important group of financial institutions also swing very widely and in a countercyclical fashion. These financiers of housing face a general policy that works against them, a policy that tends to shorten periods of expansion.

There is also the very real possibility that the recent increase in the Federal Reserve Board's emphasis on more stable growth of monetary aggregates such as the money supply may create wider and more frequent swings in interest rates than in the past. The previous approach, on the other hand, tended to stabilize interest rates by adjusting the flow of credit to changes in the demand for credit.

It is important, moreover, to note that this adversity for the major thrift institutions reaches well beyond the several thousand managers of these firms. It touches the lives of all potential borrowing customers who find that this source of credit is most abundant when they are most likely to be unemployed but much less available when they are back at work. It is also an adversity that severely limits the rewards of the principal owners and depositors of such institutions, particularly the small-scale depositors who depend most heavily on them as a safe place for their liquid savings.

Better Financing for the Financiers

It has proved very difficult to achieve monetary and fiscal policies that are even neutral toward housing, much less favorable to it. Sharp upward bursts in interest rates and a generally higher level of rates have been common features since the middle 1960s.

The intermediaries are not powerless in such circumstances. If they choose to offer higher interest rates on deposits, they will continue to attract new funds. The problem, however, is that the business of mortgage lending tends to make that course of action exceedingly expensive for private intermediaries. A large fraction of their deposits—more than three-fourths—may be withdrawn on demand or within a few months. Accordingly, higher rates on savings accounts, necessary to keep them competitive, apply to the great bulk of their deposit liabilities, whereas higher rates they might earn on the lending side will come only from *new* lending. A large fraction of mortgage lender portfolios will continue to earn at the lower yields prevalent before the capital markets tightened.

A further problem is that *current* mortgage yields do not rise as rapidly as current rates on other instruments, such as corporate bonds. As a result, even if intermediaries are able to compete for depositors' funds they will be tempted to put these funds to nonmortgage uses.

New Intermediary Arrangements

The major policy response to disintermediation has been a system of new—and in the beginning largely governmental—intermediary arrangements. The new system creates intermediation between mortgage borrowers and the *securities* market, as a supplement to intermediation between mortgage borrowers and deposit-type savers. Completely private companies have also emerged, some operating on a major scale.

It should be underscored that the new apparatus does not insulate the housing market from monetary and fiscal policy. The rise of interest rates will still discourage mortgage borrowing. Rather, the mortgage borrower now has a better chance to respond directly to swings in interest cost. Housing finance, through the new system, can compete head to head with corporate finance and government finance.

The new apparatus is built around four federal or quasi-federal institutions, with a fifth and sixth working quietly in the background, and with two major parallel thrusts in the private sector. The four at the center are the Federal Home Loan Bank System (FHLBS), the Federal Home Loan Mortgage Corporation (FHLMC), the Federal National Mortgage Association (FNMA), and the Government National Mortgage Association (GNMA). The pair in the background are the Federal Housing Authority (FHA) and the Veterans Administration (VA), which provide insurance or guarantees for mortgages meeting certain conditions.

The FHLBS includes twelve banks which operate as a credit reserve system under the supervision of the Federal Home Loan Bank Board. The members of this system are almost all savings and loan associations, and they stand in much the same relationship to the Board as commercial banks do to the Federal Reserve Board of Governors.

FHLMC, under the direction of the FHLB Board, buys and sells conventional and government-underwritten mortgages. It raises funds by selling its own obligations in the market, and by borrowing from FHLB banks or through these banks as they in turn sell securities to finance the FHLMC. FNMA is sponsored by the government but owned entirely by private stockholders. It buys and sells mortgages with the aim of creating greater liquidity in the mortgage market. GNMA, however, is entirely a government corporation, financed by funds from the U.S. Treasury. It provides money for certain types of residential mortgages as designated by law or authorized by the President. It is part of the Department of Housing and Urban Development.

While all these institutions have been in existence for some time, recent years have brought major changes in form and, for some, changes in style. As a result, a number of new links have been created between mortgage borrowers and the securities market. Moreover, the emergence of this new system of federal intermediaries has been accompanied by at least two major developments in the private sector. First, there are a number of companies that provide mortgage insurance, competing directly with the FHA and in 1972 surpassing the FHA in the volume of mortgage guarantees written. The other development is the creation by one of the private mortgage insurance companies (MGIC Investment Corporation) of a completely private competitor to FNMA. This concern ("Maggie Mae") has very quickly come to rival FNMA in the volume of funds it has provided to the secondary mortgage market.

The ability of the federal and federally sponsored agencies to create effective links between mortgage borrowers and the securities market stems from two characteristics they have in common.

One is that they package mortgages into larger bundles than the individual mortgages of the borrowing households. This is intermediation across the size gap. For some of it, the agencies issue new claims that are directly collateralized by pools of mortgages. Alternatively, they issue claims against their own generalized holdings of mortgage bundles and against the income stream produced by these assets.

The second major characteristic is the ability of these federal and quasi-federal institutions to raise funds at relatively low interest cost. For all of them, the capital market appears to perceive an implicit guarantee that the federal government stands ready to assure regular payment of both interest and principal. This confidence stems from specific insurance and guarantee commitments behind some of the issues. In others, the expectation is less concrete but nevertheless firmly held.

For several of these federal intermediary institutions, a third characteristic may be noted. It is a relative freedom from the Congressional budgetary process. Though vested with public powers, neither the Home Loan Bank System (including the FHLMC) nor FNMA is required to seek Congressional approval for the volume of debt issues they float in the securities market. Thus, their borrowing is not subject to the federal debt limit, nor is their spending included in the federal budget. This freedom has contributed markedly to their rapid growth.

Alongside the problem of disintermediation, it should be remembered, is the tendency of yields on current mortgages not to rise as sharply as rates on competing investment outlays. Thus, as capital markets tighten, private financial intermediaries often find securities such as corporate bonds more attractive than mortgage lending. As a consequence, the deposit funds that have continued to flow into financial institutions have, to some extent, been diverted to nonmortgage credit markets. This has suggested a need to improve the mortgage instrument itself, to enhance its appeal as an investment outlet.

The new apparatus of federal intermediaries makes one such improvement when it offers mortgages to institutional investors in single bundles of much larger size. The creation of these bundles, however, still requires smaller mortgage loans to be made at an earlier stage. The basic mortgage contract is not changed by the mere fact that it is later bundled with other mortgage contracts. It is still small—in mid-1972 the average price for new one-family houses financed by conventional mortgages was $27,000, with a mortgage of about $17,000.

The role played by the new network has nevertheless been very large. At their peak level in early 1970, for example, the combined loans of the Home Loan Banks and net acquisitions of mortgages by federally sponsored credit agencies was equal to more than two-thirds the net increase in residential mortgage debt. Federal support totaled $10.5 billion in mortgages at a time when the entire increase in residential mortgage debt was $15.3 billion.

The New
Network of Housing Finance

For mortgage borrowers, these innovations have opened up a much better access to the *securities* markets, and this is a major step forward. If the wide swings in the flow of housing credit can be smoothed down, the new network of public and private intermediaries can help stabilize the housing industry. It may also help to slow the rise in housing costs, by changing the entire climate in which wage and price decisions are made in the construction industry.

The new system of federal intermediation is also valuable in giving the housing market a larger, permanent access to sources of finance that have been shut off for lack of marketable instruments. Efforts have been made for many years, for example, to interest pension fund managers in residential mortgages as an investment outlet. With the transformation of mortgage loans into instruments that are tradeable in the securities markets, a breakthrough to these major sources of money may be close at hand. This technological progress in the capital and credit markets is encouraging.

Several years' experience with the new system of federal intermediation, however, has brought to the surface some serious difficulties. It is now clear that the new system will achieve a lessened volatility in mortgage supply essentially by an *alternation* between private intermediation and federal or quasi-federal intermediation. The presumption is that tight money will continue to make it hard for deposit-type institutions to compete effectively for savings flows. Accordingly, the basic strategy is for federal intermediaries, at such times, to expand their borrowing from the securities markets. What the deposit-type institutions cannot raise from *depositors,* the security-issuing institutions will raise from *investors* in the securities markets.

This characterization of the process immediately raises two major questions about the actual performance of the new system thus far. One is whether when money is tight the combined efforts of federal and private intermediaries can supply the housing market with significantly more funds than otherwise. The other is whether when money is easy the federal intermediaries, under their present rules of governance, will in fact minimize their support for private intermediary lending, as the basic strategy requires.

34.

Federal Intermediaries:
Competition in Tight Money Times

When the economy is generally booming, and interest rates are high and rising, can federal intermediaries add anything at all to the total volume of mortgage flows? Or will they simply capture, in the securities markets, funds that were induced to shift there by the higher yields being offered by federal intermediaries? Will the net result be increased disintermediation for the private institutions, with little or no increase in the amount of money going to mortgage borrowers?

One careful examination of the experience to date suggests that the access to the securities market has, indeed, increased the total flow of mortgage money.[4] The estimate is that, at most, 25 to 30 per cent of the funds raised by the government intermediaries in 1966 and in 1969 were siphoned out of the deposits of private savings institutions. On this accounting, then the new system has made a notable contribution to the stability of mortgage flows.

Such a finding, however, settles only part of the issue. One difficulty is that the evidence encompasses only limited experience with large-scale government intermediation—the experience of 1969 and the more limited support efforts of 1966. The next episode may well find many more deposit-type savers aware of these market alternatives. Their shift of allegiance in subsequent periods of credit crunch could be much sharper than in 1969.

A second concern is that even the 25 to 30 per cent of security market financing that is taken from private intermediaries can have a sharp impact on the institutions that lose those funds. The potential damage, moreover, is twofold. There is, first, the damage to the institutions as mortgage lenders. If they cannot expand at times of high interest rates, their assets will in general yield less. This will create strong incentives for them to diversify out of mortgage lending, and into other types of lending on which yields rise more rapidly in tight money times. The second damage is to the small saver who must continue to rely on time and savings deposits as the most efficient outlet available to him, given his diseconomies of scale and lack of experience in the open securities markets. When the institution at which his savings are deposited earns a lower yield, he too will earn a lower yield.

4/Leo Grebler, "Broadening the Source of Funds for Residential Mortgages," *Federal Reserve Staff Study: Ways to Moderate Fluctuations in Housing Construction* (Washington, D.C.: Board of Governors of the Federal Reserve System, December 1972).

Federal Intermediaries:
Overkill in Easy Money Times?

The basic strategy of the new system, as noted, assumes that federal intermediaries will act to *offset* the cycle in private mortgage lending. As borrowers on a very large scale, governmental intermediaries can raise funds in the securities market, an option available only to a handful of the thrift institutions. And as public agencies, with the actual or implied guarantee of the federal government standing behind their debt issues, the federal agencies can borrow at comparatively low rates. For these reasons, they are far better equipped to compete with business and other borrowers when capital markets are tight and private intermediaries are least able to fend for themselves.

A major function of federal intermediation is to raise mortgage money in tight money times. Correspondingly, when savings flow abundantly into the private thrift intermediaries, the assistance of the federal agencies is not required. Indeed, these agencies should drop back as the private institutions come forward. It is through this countervailing process that the *total* flow of mortgage credit can be made to swing less widely over the cycle.

The performance of the system in 1971 and 1972 raises serious doubt that it will *automatically* perform in this fashion. In a time of extraordinary flooding of deposit funds into savings and loan associations and savings banks and a correspondingly record flow of new mortgage money into the housing markets, the federal intermediaries did not reduce their activity. Instead, they swelled the flood with large additional amounts of mortgage credit, supplied from large, new fund-raising of their own.

Moreover, in their capacity as regulatory bodies, they have taken a number of steps in this same period to liberalize mortgage lending powers of private institutions. Some of these actions are once-over, structural changes. But they have been introduced into a market that is already unusually flush with the mortgage lending urge. This has served to push the current boom higher, and has destroyed forever the opportunity to provide such an impetus during a cyclical slump in housing.

In addition, the large volume of intermediating done in this period by the federal agencies may seriously jeopardize their ability to play that role later, when the cycle turns and housing is most in need of them. Holding so much debt already, they will be more reluctant to borrow further when borrowing rates are much higher and yields on their own portfolios are not rising proportionally. This may be particularly true for FNMA, because it is now an essentially private entity, beholden first to its stockholders and only afterward to the needs of public policy.

The Importance of Interest Rate Flexibility

We are brought by this analysis to two major sets of conclusions. They deal, first, with interest rate flexibility for the private intermediaries and, second, with the rules of governance for the federal intermediaries.

The pervasive problem of cyclical disruption makes it crucially important that the chief private suppliers of mortgage funds—the thrift institutions—be given strong incentive to keep mortgage lending at the center of their operations. We think it especially important that paramount emphasis be placed on their ability to compete as providers of mortgage credit.

For the thrift institutions to maintain their overwhelming degree of specialization in mortgage credit, however, it seems imperative that they gain greater short-term control over the interest rates that affect them most. It is crucial that when market yields begin to rise, these institutions not be locked into relatively low interest rates on either their asset side or their liability side. For if they are, they cannot defend themselves when the cycle turns against them. **To make this flexibility possible, we urge that the federal government endorse and publicize its support of private experiments with variable rate mortgages as a standard mode of doing business. We applaud the proposals of the Federal Home Loan Bank Board supporting variable rate mortgages. We recommend that similar action be taken deliberately and systematically by all agencies that buy and sell mortgages or provide direct or indirect subsidies. Precautions must be taken, however, to insure that borrowers are protected and not exploited.**

We expect that borrowers will be offered lower initial rates than those being quoted on fixed rate mortgages if they will agree to have rates move up and down with some stated index. **We recommend in particular the "variable maturity" instrument—a mortgage contract in which the rate is changed by lengthening or shortening the maturity of the mortgage, not by raising or lowering the monthly payment to be made by the**

mortgager. This will allow the lending institutions, when interest rates are rising, to treat a larger part of their monthly payment receipts as return on capital.

Lending institutions in several European nations have long made use of variable rate mortgages. In Great Britain rates on old and new mortgages tend to be changed simultaneously with deposit rates as a matter of course. These institutions, moreover, have suffered far less fluctuation in the flow of savings and mortgage credit than our savings and loan associations have, even with no British counterpart to our Federal Home Loan Bank to help them. As a further consequence, average yields on the mortgage portfolios of building societies have closely approximated current market rates on new mortgages—in sharp contrast with the American experience.

Nevertheless, the institutional setting of each country is unique. American borrowers and lenders will need to experiment with their own designs. For example, lenders would lose the stabilizing effects of the process if borrowers insisted on fixed rate mortgages when rates were low and variable rate mortgages when rates were high. Another problem in the "variable maturity" version is that the designation of a *larger* part of the fixed monthly payment as return *on* capital will mean that a correspondingly *smaller* part of the payment can be regarded as a return *of* capital—i.e., repayment of principal. Thus, a smaller quantity of these inflowing funds will be available for automatic recycling into new mortgages. Moreover, for those intermediaries that are organized as stockholder corporations rather than as mutual companies, the higher return on capital will mean a bigger tax bite. While these two shrinkages are likely to be more than fully restored by the larger flow of new deposits or capital funds that will be attracted by the higher rate of earnings, there may be lags or other unexpected quirks in the process.

A further consideration will be the ability of such mortgages to compete as investment instruments in secondary trading. This point is especially important because of the long efforts in this country to develop a strong secondary market for mortgages, to put them on equal footing as tradeable investment instruments in securities markets. Prospective purchasers of variable rate mortgages will thus be considering the alternative of putting their funds into other debt instruments (corporate bonds, for example, on which the return is fixed and known). The variable rate mortgage, by contrast, offers a much more uncertain rate of return. If this uncertainty were to make variable rate mortgages less attractive to open market investors, it would in turn make them less liquid for the institution making the initial loan.

It seems likely to us, however, that the variable rate mortgage can be made attractive to secondary market investors. First, with a debt instrument on which interest rates vary with open market rates, there will be far less tendency for the *price* of the instrument to vary. The market value of a variable rate mortgage will remain much closer to par value, regardless of interest rate fluctuations in the open market. This firmness of capital value will make variable rate mortgages more liquid than otherwise. And this tendency toward greater liquidity than is offered by other debt securities may well outweigh any opposite tendencies resulting from increased uncertainty about the size of interest rate payments.

In addition, it may be that the more apt comparison is not with alternative *debt* instruments, but with *equity* instruments. Interest rates in the open market tend to rise with general inflation in the economy. Variable rate mortgages will thus offer much the same kind of inflation hedge as common stocks offer. Indeed, it is conceivable that the introduction of variable rate mortgages will add a significant new secondary market instrument, drawing equity investment funds into debt financing. Something like this is already occurring in the development of real estate investment trusts, and this new form of mortgage could prove a further step toward tapping this additional source of funds.

Thus, design difficulties do not seem insurmountable and, in our view, are far outweighed by the fundamental advantages of variable rate mortgages. The FHA and the FHLB are already permitting such contracts, and we would urge that this kind of acknowledgement and approval be made as widely known as possible. We would also urge that wide publicity be given to the experiments of the Federal Home Loan Mortgage Corporation aimed at introducing variable rate contracts into forward commitments on multifamily units.

Indeed, we recommend that ways be sought to reward private experimentation in writing variable rate contracts—at all the various points at which federal agencies buy and sell mortgages and provide direct and indirect subsidies. Such policies of encouragement worked well when the Federal Reserve System utilized its rediscount function to foster the development of specific kinds of instruments such as bankers acceptances. Even more pertinent has been the contribution of the FHA to the development and standardization of mortgage lending practices.

In any effort to encourage the adoption of variable rate mortgages, a central question should be how best to distribute the risk of interest rate change among the different parties involved—the borrowers, the lenders, and the public at large. Under fixed rate mortgages, the lender bears all the risk of variability in market rates. The lender in this case is both the financial institution and the depositor-owner whose funds the institution is investing. We should not like to see the development of variable rate mortgages that simply shifted all this burden onto the borrowers. They are no better equipped than the lenders to bear all of it. We are proposing that the federal government encourage exploration of alternative methods of sharing the risk of interest rate changes with a concomitant federal responsibility to see that the sharing is not inequitable. It should be clearly understood that encouragement is being given to an *option*. It is important that borrowers choosing that option not have their lack of sophistication exploited.

If variable rates are introduced into new mortgages as they are written, it will take many years for these mortgages to become a major part of the intermediary portfolios. For that reason, among others, it has been suggested that, at least in the interim, financial intermediaries be offered the chance to buy insurance against the risk of interest rate changes.[5] We are inclined, however, not to endorse such a proposal. After some exploration, it appears to us that the insuring agency could not supply a meaningful amount of protection, unless it either charged a very high premium or received a very large public subsidy.

As a major step toward the interest rate flexibility necessary to keep thrift institutions viable as mortgage lenders, we urge greater flexibility of interest rate ceilings on mortgages and on savings accounts, allowing them to vary with changing market conditions. The sole purpose of such ceilings should be to set outer boundaries for safety. The ceilings, however, should interfere as little as possible with natural market forces.

The FHA and VA ceilings on interest rates are a dampening force because they always pose the threat of making the cyclical rise in mortgage rates still more sluggish than it already is. Yet there is very little evidence that these ceilings, and particularly those of the FHA, provide an

---

5/See Edward E. Edwards, "Insurance Against Interest Rate Risk in Home Mortgage Lending," background paper for the President's Commission on Financial Structure and Regulation (the Hunt Commission); and Robert Lindsay, "Rate-Risk Insurance for Mortgage Lenders," *Federal Reserve Staff Study: Ways to Moderate Fluctuations in Housing Construction* (Washington, D.C.: Board of Governors of the Federal Reserve System, December 1972).

overriding benefit to the borrower. **As an interim step toward lifting the FHA and VA ceilings entirely and holding them in a standby status, the agencies should be permitted to adopt the dual rate proposed several years ago by the Commission on Mortgage Interest Rates.** Under this system, lenders and borrowers in writing FHA and VA mortgages could choose between two arrangements. They could stick with the present arrangement under which the contract rate must not exceed the stated ceiling but the lender can charge discount points up to some stated number. Alternatively, they could negotiate freely the interest rate, with no discounts permitted. As an experiment this would give valuable insight into the effects of taking off the ceiling, but meanwhile provide the present protection to borrowers who did not wish to be part of an experiment.

The state usury ceilings on mortgage rates create a separate problem because they cannot be changed administratively. **Where it does not seem feasible to remove such ceilings entirely, we urge that they be raised well above the average mortgage rates of recent years.** This would deter exploitation of the unwary by the unscrupulous—the major objective of such ceilings—without unduly dampening the flow of mortgage credit between the main body of borrowers and lenders. We also expect that experience with the dual rate at the federal level will suggest new possibilities for greater rate flexibility within a fixed-rate system. And we suggest that support for the federal dual rate could perhaps be recruited at the state level, to give the federal experiment a broader base and a more likely spillover into new state legislation.

It is necessary, in our view, for thrift institutions to be both able and willing to raise the interest rates they pay for deposits—their dividend rates—when money and capital markets tighten. Otherwise, they will not escape disintermediation. Moreover, there will be little point in arranging for their interest rate revenues to rise with market rates, if they do not use these added revenues to hold their deposit customers by offering them higher returns. Indeed, flexibility in mortgage rates is not defensible as public policy if the higher earnings cannot be shared with depositors.

In time, such ceilings should be lifted completely if experience with the full assortment of new financial tools and instruments warrants such change. Even then, however, standby authority should be maintained to reimpose interest rate ceilings if necessary.

Implementation of this set of recommendations should help assure the continued, long-term viability of the $350 billion "thrift institutions" —the savings and loan associations and mutual savings banks—which are by far the most important source of mortgage lending money. We recognize, however, that these recommendations will not provide a rapid solution to the problem of cyclical disruption since it will take time before variable rate mortgages bceome a significant part of loan portfolios, and even then such mortgages might be spread unevenly among the thrift institutions.

Rules of Governance for the Federal Agencies

There are two justifications for granting special authority to the federal and quasi-federal intermediaries. One is technological efficiency, the ability to assemble and package a product on a scale and in a form that will reach new customers. The other is the social interest vested in the activities being financed.

The resulting power given to the federal intermediaries, however, may inadvertently create large-scale disintermediation at the private financial institutions. Of special concern is the ambiguous role of FNMA, a government corporation owned by private stockholders, with shares traded in the stock market. In some future period of capital market stringency, the management of FNMA might well conclude that the best interests of its stockholders would be served by issuing a large volume of short-term notes. If so, and again in the best interests of the shareholders, it could be expected to put energetic and imaginative people to work on the design and marketing of those issues. With the implicit guarantee of the federal government also stamped on the resulting product, funds might come tumbling out of the deposit-type mortgage-lending private institutions.

We are also concerned over the demonstrated tendency of these agencies to continue their expansionary actions into periods of slack capital markets.

More generally, we are concerned about the possibility of an excessive proliferation of independent borrowing authorities at both the federal and state levels. This development raises two possible dangers.

One is that the process may soon be self-defeating. As more and more public borrowers enter the capital markets on a vast scale to intermediate between lenders and other borrowers, the spread between the borrowing and lending rates of these public agencies will narrow.

Their technological efficiency will be dissipated. As this occurs, the agencies risk the loss of their self-sustaining status. They risk becoming public wards, with their obligations becoming direct claims on the nation's *tax* revenues.

The other danger is that even if no such evil befalls the federal intermediaries, they will nevertheless have a major allocation effect in the meantime. Without being subjected to the normal checks and balances of the governmental process, they will have routed enormous amounts of public money into particular uses.

To reduce these dangers, we repeat our earlier endorsement of the proposed Federal Financing Bank to coordinate federal agency borrowing and guarantee programs.[6] We recommend, as we did in our previous statement, that the President be authorized to place limits on the total volume of loan guarantees and of borrowing by federal and federally sponsored credit agencies. These limitations should be subject to Congressional review and should extend to all government sponsored credit agencies (including those, like FNMA, that are privately owned) which benefit from an implied federal guarantee of their securities.

We urge that a clear set of guidelines be developed for the federal intermediaries, setting out as precisely as possible their roles and responsibilities as part of a coherent national housing policy.

The federal intermediaries, of course, do not operate in a policy vacuum. Their activities are affected to a major degree by the actions of other government agencies. From time to time, these actions conflict with each other—sometimes inevitably, sometimes unnecessarily. It is therefore essential to have a single organizational framework which can deal with the inherent conflict between countercyclical policy for housing and stabilization policy for the economy in general.

To develop and coordinate the implementation of internally consistent policies, a formal mechanism is needed that will draw all the federal and quasi-federal housing agencies into the monetary and fiscal policy decision-making process of the federal government. We recommend that the informal committees of recent administrations be succeeded by a formal, systematic council within the Executive Branch.

It is especially important that housing not be made the principal vehicle of general monetary policy restraint. The guidelines should assure

6/ *High Employment Without Inflation: A Positive Program for Economic Stabilization,* A Statement on National Policy by the Research and Policy Committee, Committee for Economic Development (July 1972).

that credit restrictions do not fall unduly on any one sector. When monetary policy decisions are made, the cyclical problems of housing should receive special attention because of their great severity.

We also recommend that the guidelines to federal agencies make clear, and mandatory, the responsibility of the federal housing intermediaries for concentrating their assistance in periods when the private institutions are experiencing most difficulty in attracting savings deposits.

The conflict is especially troublesome when the economy is weak. At such times, mortgage financing is likely to be most available and housing activity most vigorous. It is also at such times, however, that the temptation is greatest to use the special powers of the federal credit agencies to stimulate housing even further. Yielding to such temptation will worsen the already wide fluctuations in housing activity.

We urge the enactment of legislation mandating the federal and quasi-federal housing intermediaries to act to counter the cycle in housing activity and to narrow its amplitude, not to encourage wider swings up or down.

These recommendations are not aimed at shifting the pattern of the housing cycle to make it coincide with fluctuations in the general economy, but rather are designed to smooth down the amplitude of the housing cycle. Their effect would be twofold. First, they would make it easier for thrift institutions to ride out the storm of fluctuations in interest rates. And, second, they would clearly orient federal intermediation to work chiefly as a counterforce to private disintermediation.

Chapter 3
· · · · · · · · · · · · · ·
Housing Finance
for the Housing Poor

U nlike the problems discussed in
the previous chapter, housing poverty persists through all phases of the
business cycle. Although the nation has wrestled with the problem for
many years and launched a major new attack with the Housing and
Urban Development Act of 1968, the United States has never directed
a sufficient volume of financial resources toward its alleviation. The
problem is thus far from solved. There is, in fact, widespread agreement
today that present housing programs are inadequate.

In ordinary usage, the housing problems of the poor are not
financing problems. They are income problems.[1] Families of low income
cannot purchase decent housing at market prices and still have much
income left for other necessities. The most direct response of public policy
would be to provide more income or to provide greater opportunities to
earn more income.

1/They may also be *social* problems, but many of these also stem from long-term inadequacies of income.

Over a number of years, however, the nation has attempted to treat these needs financially through a variety of credit subsidies combined with a strategy known as "filtering." Under some recent programs, the credit subsidy goes directly to the household as owner of the dwelling place. In the great bulk of programs, the credit is an indirect subsidy, supplied to builders and landlords and even to mortgage lenders. Either way, the cost of housing services is reduced for the ultimate consumer, the occupant.

For many families, credit subsidies have proved to be fully as effective in achieving better housing conditions as income supplements would have been. In all such cases, however, at least two conditions must be present for the credit subsidy to succeed. One is that the occupant families must have enough income to pay the housing costs (including the debt service) not covered by the credit subsidy. The other condition is that these other expenses of providing housing services must not rise faster than the tenant's ability to pay.

Yet by various measures of housing poverty, a significant number of families has not had incomes large enough or dependable enough for them to afford decent housing, even if the financing to builders and landlords had been supplied at *zero* rates of interest. It also appears that in the 1960s the costs of operating and maintaining rental housing in large urban centers increased more rapidly than the rents that the available tenants in a large part of the stock were willing or able to pay.

Moreover, credit assistance has been concentrated overwhelmingly in the construction of new housing. The assumption underlying such a policy is that new houses will release older housing, which in turn will "filter" down to levels the poor can afford. The older structures, often in less fashionable neighborhoods, cannot command the relative prices or rents they once did. With a flow of new units added to the nation's housing stock, the older units will begin the filtering process earlier than they would have without the new housing. Thus the poor are served indirectly with older but inhabitable houses.

If this filtering process is to work, however, it must perform two distinct and very difficult tasks. First, the provision of new housing must start a filtering chain that ultimately eliminates from the housing stock the units which are least inhabitable. In addition, the construction of new housing must release livable used housing into markets that will in fact make such housing available to the families of lowest income. All these markets must work so that the poor vacate the substandard housing,

46.

permitting it to go off the market completely, and then move into the used housing left empty by the moderate-income families who are relocating into the new construction.

For these various filterings to work as expected, the markets necessary to the process must work well. In addition, either the families at the bottom must have sufficient income or potential landlord owners of the buildings being filtered must have some other assurances of revenue.

In our view, this combined strategy of credit subsidies and filtering has not worked well. Housing poverty in this eighth decade of the twentieth century is still far too common.

The Incidence of Housing Poverty

The magnitude of housing poverty is commonly measured in two ways — by a physical standard and by an income standard.

The Condition of Housing Units. As measured by the official definition, the incidence of substandard housing dropped significantly during the 1950s and the 1960s. By 1970 substandard housing had come to be less than 8 per cent for the nation as a whole. Moreover, the improvement occurred in all sectors, both inside and outside SMSAS and in all major regions, benefiting both nonwhite occupants and whites.

Nevertheless, nonwhites and families living outside the SMSAS still suffer a relatively high incidence of substandard housing. For example, for all the improvement in the 1960s and earlier, a nonwhite family living outside a metropolitan area still had, at the beginning of the 1970s, a less than even chance of occupying quarters classified as meeting minimum physical standards.

In all, about 4.8 million families could be classified in 1970 as housing poor because their dwellings were dilapidated or did not have adequate plumbing facilities.

Acting conservatively, we can also identify another 4.0 million households as housing poor because of overcrowding (more than one person per room) in otherwise acceptable quarters. Thus, the measure of housing poverty is raised to 8.8 million households, representing about one out of seven households in the nation. Black families, it should be noted, account for about 2.3 million within that total, or roughly 2½ times what their numbers in the total population would predict.

Housing and Ability to Pay. A separate way of identifying the housing poor is to examine the portion of income absorbed by payments for shelter. It may be that standard quality housing, though available to the poor, is very expensive for them. Even housing in poor physical condition may take a big chunk out of income. In either case, the consequence would be more crowding and/or a greater pressure to skimp on other necessities.

For both renters and owner-occupants, the lower the income the bigger the bite taken for payments for housing. (See Appendix Table B-3.) But this evidence is ambiguous because it takes no account of other needs. For some low-income families the bite may be less painful because the family is small and has lower expenses for food, clothing and other necessities.

An alternative measure can be derived by using the yardstick budgets developed by the Bureau of Labor Statistics for four-person families in urban areas. In the spring of 1967, the shelter budget for a "lower living standard" averaged $1,013 for all the urban United States. This paid for rental housing that met the "basic requirement for health" and did not cover even the minimum of household operation and house furnishing. The very lowest figure for any reported city was $770 ($64 per month) in Austin, Texas. By the fall of 1971, it had risen to an estimated $928 ($77 per month).

From this base can be estimated the number of families that are housing poor by a range of income standards. A rough measure of this number can be inferred from various assumptions about the maximum percentage of income that "ought" to go into housing. Assuming an upper limit of 25 per cent, for example, annual rent payments of $928 imply an income of $3,713. (See Appendix Table B-4.) In 1971 there were about 13 million households with incomes at or below that level.

From this crude measure, it seems reasonable once again to suppose that something like one out of seven households must be classified as housing poor. Indeed, taking the computation at face value, the incidence of housing poverty is greater than one out of seven. The computation is based on the least expensive city in the national sample, and even on that low base the cost of housing would take more than 25 per cent of the income of every sixth family in the country. Hence, one-seventh seems a conservative measure.

Again, black families are represented disproportionately, but somewhat less so than with physical measures of housing quality.

48.

The Present Program

As noted, the federal government has attempted to assist low-income families chiefly through the finance markets. It has helped to provide credit, not income. Moreover, the credit has been available almost exclusively for *new production,* not for the utilization of older, secondhand housing that was originally constructed outside the government programs, with other sources of finance. The federal subsidy programs have attempted to meet the demand of low- and middle-income families largely by helping to create new supply.

Assistance to the lowest income families is provided through public housing authorities, which issue bonds and use the proceeds to build rental facilities. The interest and principal on these bonds is then paid by the federal government as it falls due over the years. Freed from this expense, housing authorities can offer apartments at rentals about half the market rate. The program continues, but its growth is currently much overshadowed by subsidized programs for moderate income families. (See Appendix A on Federal Housing Subsidies.) Moreover, inflation in recent years has created great difficulties for many public housing authorities in the management of housing constructed in earlier years.

Some used housing is acquired in this way, but the total was less than one-fifth of all units added to the program in fiscal 1969 and 1970. It was even smaller, both absolutely and proportionately, in fiscal 1971 and 1972.

The other subsidy aid to the poor—*rent supplements*—comes nearest to "financing" the demand side. It is a relatively small program, however, and purchases no used housing at all. Indeed, the objective is to induce new construction, under the sponsorship of nonprofit organizations, cooperatives, or limited-dividend corporations. The subsidy is tied to the finished building and fills the gap between (a) market rentals and (b) one-quarter of a family's gross income (minus $300 for each dependent). The tenant's income must be low enough to qualify for public housing. But, if family incomes rise faster than market rents, the subsidy payments decline. If market rates move up faster than the tenant's ability to pay, the sponsors receive a cash subsidy to meet the need.

Programs for moderate-income families originated in the so-called Section 221(d)(3) program which provided low-interest loans directly to housing owners, who could then offer below-market rental rates. The program is now being phased out in favor of the two other approaches—Section 235 and 236 loans. In both these newer programs, the loans come from private lending institutions, instead of directly from the government. The subsidy is built around interest rate levels. Borrowers get low interest loans and the private lenders get the going market rate. The government subsidy fills the gap.

With Section 235 the nation adopted its first major program of direct subsidy for private *homeownership*. The aid subsidizes more than the interest rate alone, but nonetheless is geared to interest rate differences. The maximum subsidy is set by computing the difference between the monthly carrying charges, including payment of principal, on (a) a mortgage rate of 1 per cent and on (b) a mortgage with the market rate actually being charged. The government then pays the mortgage lender whatever part of that gap cannot be filled from 20 per cent of the homeowner's income. Thus, at a minimum, the homeowner must be able to carry a 1 per cent mortgage, and he must do so on one-fifth of his income. Moreover, since he must also operate and maintain the home, his monthly expenses will also include taxes, heat, light, electricity, and the rest.

The Section 236 program applies the same basic idea to multi-family units. The project sponsors charge rents at one-fourth of a tenant's income (minus $300 for each minor). From the rent proceeds, they pay the 1 per cent debt service and the operating and maintenance cost. Anything remaining goes to the government.

The support received by individual families in these two programs is considerable. Yet because the recipients themselves must be able to finance a significant fraction of the housing cost, the subsidies are available mostly to families whose incomes are well above the poverty level.

Within the last year, the subsidy programs have come under considerable attack, particularly those employed in inner-city areas, such as the Section 221(d)(3), 235 and 236 programs. The most widely voiced complaints have been set off by the discovery of dishonesty and fraud in the implementation of the programs, leading to a number of indictments in several major cities.

A second major criticism has centered on cost. Part of this concern stems from the high per unit cost of subsidized construction. Another part reflects the losses the government will sustain on the large number of houses it must now repossess, after fraudulent overvaluation in the subsidy process. Still another cost complaint focuses on the large volume of funds that will be required over the long period—forty years or more —that a mortgage support program necessarily entails.

50.

The third set of criticisms has raised doubts about the effectiveness of the programs in serving the nation's most pressing housing needs. Former Secretary of Housing and Urban Development George Romney, for example, has said that subsidies are hurting the inner cities more than they are helping them, by financing the flight of the middle class.* Others have voiced serious misgivings about the effectiveness of any program that simultaneously seeks to increase housing and decrease poverty; they fear that such programs may in the end accomplish neither of these objectives or do so only in a most inefficient manner.

We see no reason for believing that fraud is inherent in the design of these housing subsidies. It seems more likely to us that the abuses stem from the unusually rapid buildup in the programs and a failure to develop the necessary reorientation in administrative practices.

We consider it particularly unfortunate that the task of administering subsidies for low- and middle-income families — programs with a "social" purpose—should have fallen on a staff trained for a very different kind of underwriting responsibility. The FHA, the agency in question, was required in the process to take on a double role. In addition to its traditional focus on the quality of loans—the concern of the lender—it was also required to assume responsibility for housing cost and housing quality—the concern of the borrower. This expansion of responsibility has proved difficult, and corruption and graft have appeared.

We agree that it is difficult for the same staff members to perform adequately these two opposite roles. We believe, however, that these separate responsibilities can be discharged satisfactorily by separate departments of the same agency. The problem is administrative.

The traditional FHA function of providing mortgage guarantees for higher-income families has in recent years been taken over to a large extent by private mortgage insurance firms. Consequently, it has been suggested that the FHA should be entirely relieved of this responsibility and should focus all its attention on the subsidy programs. We do not believe, however, that the private firms will be able to supply profitably all the mortgage insurance that should be made available in the light of national policy goals. We therefore recommend that the FHA retain responsibility for providing both mortgage guarantees to higher-income families and credit assistance to moderate- and low-income households. It must, of course, also receive sufficient funding to meet its important staff needs in both these areas.

---

*See Memorandum by MR. ROBERT C. WEAVER, page 58.

Much of the concern over the cost of housing subsidies also seems to us to be overdrawn. The total expense of a program over forty years old is bound to be large, and by itself is not a helpful measure of the burden to be borne. Although savings should not be achieved by building housing barracks of substandard architectural design, every effort should be made to keep unit costs at reasonable levels. We are especially concerned about the frequent failure of the subsidy programs to provide assistance to those who need it the most. We believe that there is a need for a restructuring of the basic design of housing policy.

The Need for Change

It is clear from the considerable incidence of housing poverty that the quantity of adequate housing available to low- and middle-income families must be made larger. It also seems to us that an increased availability of such housing requires a significant amount of new construction. Thus, in our judgment, the nation should continue to subsidize the building of new housing for low- and middle-income families.

We come to this conclusion because:

1) It is evident that the filtering process does not work well enough to provide the poor with enough quality housing at prices they can afford.

2) The spread of the abandonment process means, among other things, that the market is failing to keep in use even some good housing that has already filtered down to low-income families.

3) Particularly in large urban areas, it is important not to have a policy that condemns low-income families automatically to live in the oldest and maybe the worst parts of the city.

These considerations also suggest, however, the need for major changes in the program by which new construction is currently subsidized. They also point up the weaknesses of a housing strategy that puts all its emphasis on the supply side, virtually ignoring the problems on the demand side. We need a strategy that addresses itself to both supply and demand.

For improving the supply strategy, we urge the following changes.

In our opinion, a major weakness of the present subsidy program is the income level of the families being assisted most directly. The chief

52.

recipients of Section 235 and 236 loans, the programs with greatest momentum, are not those most in need. Implicitly, the current design of the housing subsidy program assumes a filtering process that is not at all likely to occur.

We therefore urge a major shift in the allocation of subsidies for low-income families. A much larger share of the public subsidy for housing must be channeled to those at the bottom of the income ladder.

We also emphasize the importance of providing greater amenities in low-income housing programs. If the point of these programs is to help draw the poor into the mainstream of American life, it makes no sense to offer them housing that obviously brands them as outsiders. Prudent expenditure of public funds does not require that apartment buildings be barracks. Moreover, if such ventures should later fail as public housing projects, they cannot then be made to succeed as private ventures. Adding amenities afterwards is far too expensive.

In addition, we urge a greater effort to increase supply by drawing used housing into the stock that is made available to low-income families. We recognize that in many cases this would serve only to bid up the price without adding to the supply. We are encouraged, however, by the possibility that in local markets that are slack, public subsidies can provide quarters for low-income families at much lower cost than new construction would require. Much greater use should be made of the leasing program.

On the demand side, the problem, of course, is inadequate income. The difficulty is the "financing" of occupancy. We therefore urge that much greater thought be given to this strand of housing strategy.

**We strongly support a large-scale, national program providing housing allowances directly to low-income families.*

Such a program would provide eligible households with the means to pay for the estimated cost of adequate housing. Households would be required to pay a specified percentage—about one-fourth—of their income for rent. The housing allowance in turn would provide the difference between this sum and the shelter costs for units which meet a minimum specified level of adequacy.

The cost of such a housing allowance at the present level of assistance to the housing poor need not be any greater than subsidies in their present form and may well be less. Of course, extension of housing allowances to all families who might be deemed eligible under present

*See Memorandum by MR. E. SHERMAN ADAMS. page 57.

standards (such as the households who are now on waiting lists for public housing) would add significantly to the cost of a housing allowance program, just as the direct provision of housing to such families would greatly increase the cost of present programs. Under current economic and budgetary conditions, however, the housing allowance program must be designed and implemented so that a significant inflationary impact is avoided and excessive pressure is not placed on the federal budget.*

Because much remains to be learned about the impact and the most effective means of mounting and administering housing allowance programs, we endorse the systematic experimentation already begun by federal agencies. These experiments are needed *not* for deciding whether the country should have such programs, but rather for determining how best to design them.

We recommend, moreover, that in these experiments a serious effort be made to discover methods by which low-income occupants can be provided with both the means and the motivation for maintaining the houses and neighborhoods in which they live. Such methods might include, for example, the provision of allowances for repairs and replacements, and homeownership counseling for families with no experience of their own to draw upon. We also urge vigorous experiments aimed at developing programs under which low-income renters would be able gradually to acquire equity ownership in the homes they occupy.

For the foreseeable future, we recommend that income supplements be tied directly to housing, including used as well as new housing. Ultimately, these income supplements should be incorporated into the more general programs of income maintenance, with the recipients free to allocate the funds according to their own priorities.[3] Even within this freedom of choice, the size of payments might be varied in different parts of the country, to take account of regional differentials in housing costs. Ideally and ultimately, the level of income supplements would be high enough everywhere to permit the recipients flexibility in allocating the funds. It should be very clear, however, that moving to this stage will require much higher levels of income maintenance than in any of the programs currently being debated.

Until housing allowances are a reality on a large scale, subsidies provided through the building of new houses should be continued. They

---

3/*Improving the Public Welfare System,* A Statement on National Policy by the Research and Policy Committee, Committee for Economic Development (April 1970).

*See Memorandum by MR. DAVIDSON SOMMERS, page 57.

should not be cut back while the housing allowance experiments are taking place. If the pace of new construction is not increased or at least maintained at current levels, the growth in the housing stock will fall significantly behind the need. For one thing, the population continues to grow and move. Moreover, until we can learn how to stem the large-scale abandonment of physically sound housing in many central cities, the high levels of abandonment will require still further growth in the housing stock.*

Once an effective design of housing allowances has been selected, the construction subsidies can be phased down as the housing allowance program takes effect. However, even after the housing allowance program is fully established, some minimal subsidies to new construction may continue to be necessary.*

Whatever the form, housing assistance for low-income families should not be confined to the older, more urban areas. While urban life has vibrance and excitement and special cultural advantages, the suburbs offer major advantages of their own, including better funding of local schools and hospitals, and sometimes better jobs and better access to power and status in the society at large. The important need is a greater range of choice for low-income families. In some localities this will require subsidies for the construction of new housing.*

In sum, because the markets work so poorly for the poor, financial assistance must be provided. It must at the same time produce more housing units and make possible more consumption of housing services.

---

*See Memoranda by MR. ROBERT C. WEAVER, pages 57 and 58.

Memoranda of Comment, Reservation, or Dissent

Page 10—By R. STEWART RAUCH, JR.:

I do not approve this policy statement because the new housing proposals of the Administration make the contents of this statement no longer pertinent.

Page 10—By H. C. TURNER, JR.:

An important factor in the rapid deterioration of substantial housing structures in inner-city neighborhoods is the great increase of vandalism of these structures when they become vacant, and due to the increased crime in the neighborhood. Local authorities must find a way to combat and eradicate these factors.

Page 11—By OSCAR A. LUNDIN:

This policy statement provides a good over-view of some of the financing problems encountered in attempting to make the nation's housing laws more responsive to the needs of all sectors of our society. In my judgment, however, the paper fails to provide adequate solutions to these problems and does not establish a framework of priorities within which the problems may be evaluated. In a number of instances the statement does not give sufficient direction even with respect to the limited issues to which the paper addresses itself. Recommendations that "guidelines should be established" seem inadequate, particularly if it is not entirely clear by whom the guidelines should be established or, as a matter of fact, whether guidelines can be formulated to accomplish the stated objectives. For these reasons I have serious reservations about the policy procedures advanced.

Pages 20 and 53—By E. SHERMAN ADAMS:

This proposal for a large-scale, national program providing housing allowances directly to low-income families is perhaps the most important recommendation in the CED statement. I only wish that every member of Congress and everyone else who is at all concerned about the housing problems of this nation would read carefully the sections of this statement which deal with the problem of housing poverty and would take this main message to heart. Year after year, decade after decade, it has been repeatedly demonstrated that the "filtering" theory simply does not work adequately. It is hard to see how anyone who reviews the facts and reasoning presented in this statement could help agreeing that there must be a massive shift of public policy to channel a much larger share of housing subsidies directly to those who desperately need them.

Pages 21 and 54—By DAVIDSON SOMMERS, with which HOWARD S. TURNER
has asked to be associated:

It is essential that federal programs, including housing programs, be integrated into an overall budgetary stance that is appropriate to current and foreseeable economic circumstances and consistent with the full-employment-balance in the budget supported by CED. I assume that CED's sponsorship of the present study is to be understood as being qualified by this basic constraint. Otherwise, the benefits to housing afforded by specific government programs may be lost in the adverse impact on the general housing market of inflation and credit crunches.

Pages 22 and 55—By ROBERT C. WEAVER:

It should be recognized, too, that production oriented subsidies for new or rehabilitated low- and moderate-income housing serve identifiable social objectives. If urban renewal areas are to provide shelter for varied income groups or for low- and moderate-income households, these subsidies are necessary. The same is true if many blighted central city areas are to be upgraded into viable neighborhoods.

Pages 22 and 55—By ROBERT C. WEAVER:

There are many uncertainties as to the impact and operation of housing allowances. This is why there is advocacy of experiments. One of the primary objectives of the latter is to discover the impact of housing allowances upon the supply and consumer cost of standard low- and moderate-income housing. Thus, it is premature to decree that minimal subsidies to new construction may be required. Both housing assistance and production subsidies will be needed. I anticipate that the mix will depend upon the composition of the housing market involved and its vacancy rates by price and size categories. The need for subsidies to new construction may well be more than minimal.

Pages 22 and 55—By ROBERT C. WEAVER:

Many suburbs do not have a supply of shelter which would be within the financial reach of lower-income families even if the latter received reasonably liberal housing allowances. Thus, if urban low- and moderate-income families are not to be restricted to the older suburbs, production oriented subsidies are needed. Although this is implied in the text, it needs to be set forth more explicitly.

Page 51—By ROBERT C. WEAVER:

The reference here is to subsidies and applicable to both housing allowances (with probably greater intensity) and to production oriented subsidies for lower-income households. In the context of discussing the relative efficacy of the two forms of subsidy, it seems irrelevant.

Appendices
· · · · · · · · · · · · · · ·
A: Federal
Housing Subsidies

The most readily measured housing subsidies are the federal programs designed specifically to assist families of low or moderate income. Less easy to measure, but no less important, are the several other federal subsidies that are implicit in the income tax system, in the federal guarantees or insurance for private mortgage loans, and in the "new system" of federal intermediation aimed at enlarging the flow of capital market funds into the mortgage market.

Starting with the *direct* subsidies for low- and moderate-income families, a first indication of their magnitude and nature is the number of additional housing units these programs make available each year. Most of these units are newly constructed or newly rehabilitated. Some, however, are leased or purchased from the existing supply, without significant renovation, to make them more accessible to families the programs are designed to reach.

By this general measure, the recent and projected magnitudes are shown in Table 1. The level of subsidized production has moved up sharply. The steepest advances, both absolutely and proportionately, have been in the rental assistance (Section 236) and homeownership (Section 235) programs, the major new thrust to come out of the Housing and Urban Development Act of 1968. Both are also projected to grow still

Table 1: Federally Subsidized Housing Production and Subsidized Use of Existing Units Fiscal Years 1969-1973

New Production Units	1969	1970	1971	1972 (est.)	1973 (est.)
Public housing	69,510	89,340	96,590	60,000	65,000
Rent supplement	16,640	22,530	16,810	14,000	20,000
Home ownership (235)	7,980	70,180	137,590	141,000	165,000
Rental assistance (236)	44,590	78,250	118,610	151,500	176,000
Rural housing	35,750	51,210	85,590	91,600	115,300
Other miscellaneous	17,140	17,940	24,620	11,100	11,000
TOTAL CONSTRUCTION	191,610	329,450	479,810	469,200	552,300

Existing Housing Units	1969	1970	1971	1972 (est.)	1973 (est.)
Public housing	18,140	13,630	8,930	7,000	35,000
Home ownership	3,020	24,530	11,720	18,000	20,600
Rural housing	10,130	14,970	20,060	22,200	26,700
TOTAL USED HOUSING UNITS	31,290	53,130	40,710	47,200	82,300

Source: President of the United States, *Fourth Annual Report on National Housing Goals* (June 29, 1972), pp. 44, 47.

larger. By contrast, the two programs designed for the poor—public housing and rent supplements—have had a more modest expansion, and the record for rent supplements can hardly be called an expansion at all. It should be added, however, that construction of new public housing units had begun several years ago to climb, and the level reached in 1971 was almost triple the annual figures before 1967. Even so, the projections show that the main growth in subsidized production in the near future is to be centered in the program for low- and moderate-income families above the poverty line.

Putting an annual monetary value on these various subsidies is somewhat more difficult. The direct budget outlays by the federal government can be measured readily enough, and rose from $1.46 billion in fiscal 1971 to an estimated $1.82 billion in fiscal 1972 and an expected $2.33 billion in fiscal 1973. But this misses much of the monetary value that the subsidies have for the beneficiaries of the programs. Each new unit brought under subsidy represents a commitment by the federal government to make payments not only in the initial year but over a number of future years as well. The inducement being offered to the producer of a new unit, and to its ultimate owner, includes this promise by the government to pay future sums of money, whether in interest or principal or some combination of both. The subsidy incentive is thus also spread into the future. The ultimate beneficiary of the subsidy must of course await the passing of these years before receiving the full subsidy flow, but the promise has a present value that induces action in the present which might otherwise not be forthcoming. Accordingly, the subsidy provided in any one year can be stated as the present value of the new flow of payments committed by the government in that year.

Recent efforts by the staff of the Joint Economic Committee of Congress have provided us with estimates of the general order of magnitude of present values of these subsidies for the fiscal year 1970. Using the same groupings as above, the gross budgetary costs of these programs are given in Table 2.

It should be underscored that these figures provide only a general order of magnitude, and our use of these estimates does not necessarily imply endorsement of the estimates or of the underlying methodology. As with any other calculation of present values, there are difficulties in selecting the most appropriate interest rate by which to discount the future sums (or, in alternative language, to capitalize those future flows into the form of a present value). Further, in some of the programs,

Table 2: Present Value of Gross Budgetary Cost of Federal Housing Credit Subsidies in Fiscal Year 1970 (in millions of dollars)

Public housing	1,064 ⎫	
Rent supplement	163 ⎭	1,227
Home ownership (235)	426 ⎫	
Rental assistance (236)	859 ⎭	1,285
Rural housing		136
Other miscellaneous		65
TOTAL		2,713

the future payments to be made by the government are not fixed, but will change with changes in the income of occupants, the operating costs of owners, and interest rates in the open market.

As these figures indicate, the federal government provides about the same subsidies for moderate- and low-income families (in the 235 and 236 programs) as for those further down the income ladder (in public housing and rent supplement units). Since these estimates are based on commitments made in 1970, they do not reflect the shifting emphasis among the different programs noted above.

A different form of subsidy is offered by the federal government through the income tax system. Taxpayers living in their own homes are permitted to deduct mortgage interest payments and real estate tax payments in computing their federal income tax liability. Further, owners of rental housing may take depreciation allowances, and there are also tax subsidies for rehabilitation expenditures on low-income housing.

The Joint Economic Committee study has attempted to calculate as well the total size of these *tax subsidies*. For illustration of general orders of magnitude, the JEC's estimates for fiscal 1970 are shown in Table 3. They totalled about $5.7 billion, almost entirely in the form of tax deductions for owner-occupants. These tax subsidies were thus more than twice as large as the present value of the credit subsidies.

62.

Table 3: Gross Budgetary Cost
of Federal Subsidies to Housing in Fiscal Year 1970
(in millions of dollars)

Federal housing credit subsidies (present value)		2,713
Tax subsidies		
Deductability of interest on owner-occupied homes	2,600	
Deductability of property taxes on owner-occupied homes	2,800	
Depreciation of rental housing	275	
Rehabilitation of low-income housing	5	
Total Tax Subsidies		5,680
TOTAL FEDERAL SUBSIDIES		
Not including imputed rent exclusion		8,393
Imputed net rent—1966 estimate		4,000
Including imputed rent exclusion		12,393

It is sometimes suggested that taxpayers living in their own homes get a further subsidy because they receive an *imputed* income from their homes, on which they pay no tax at all. If they had invested the same funds in assets that earned a money income, according to this line of thinking, they would have to pay federal taxes on that income. The Joint Economic Committee study treats this exemption of income in kind as a tax subsidy, but makes no estimate of the 1970 monetary value of it. Instead it notes that an estimate by Henry Aaron for 1966 put the subsidy at about $4.0 billion.[1]

1/"Income Taxes and Housing," *American Economic Review* (December 1960).

The *distribution of housing subsidies by income brackets* for direct subsidy programs is indicated in the upper half of Table 4. The years shown are not all the same because of data availability. But the general pattern is clear. All of the programs are concentrated almost entirely on households with less than $10,000 in annual income. For the programs in the columns at the right-hand side of the table, which in numbers of new units are the largest and fastest growing, the bulk of the benefits goes to families with incomes of $4,000 to $8,000. Though rental assistance does reach down somewhat below the poverty line, the chief aid for poverty families comes from public housing and rent supplements.

The lower half of Table 4 relates these distributions of benefits by income to the distribution of all households by income. If the portion of benefits received by any given bracket were exactly the same as the portion of all households falling into that bracket, the entry for the bracket would be zero. Thus, a negative sign indicates that the income bracket is getting less than its "share" of the benefits, and a positive sign that it is getting more than its "share."

For distribution of federal income tax subsidies by income brackets, a useful measure is provided in President Nixon's Fourth Annual Report on National Housing Goals, issued in mid-1972. The report estimates that in 1971 the allowance of mortgage interest and property tax payments by homeowners reduced federal revenues by $4.7 billion. It adds that "no comparable tax benefits exist for occupants of rental housing, although they may benefit from lower rentals if the property owners shift forward some of their tax savings."

A table provided in the President's Report, and shown here in adapted form as Table 5, makes clear that, as the Report says, "such subsidies are worth relatively more to higher income homeowners." As may be seen in Column (4) of Table 5, the dollar volume of these deductions is concentrated in upper income levels, with about two-fifths of the total going to taxpayers with adjusted gross income of $20,000 or more. Column (5) indicates that the benefits received by taxpayers in the higher brackets are several times as large as they would be if benefits in each income bracket were proportionate to the number of taxpayers in each bracket.

64.

Table 4: Distribution by Income Brackets of Benefits from Federally Subsidized Housing Production (per cent)

Annual Income	Public Housing[a]	Rent Supplements[b]	Rental Assistance[c]	Home Ownership[d]	Rural Housing[b]
Under $2,000	32.4	48.8	—	} 5.3	—
$2,000-4,000	43.0	44.3	24.2		10.7
$4,000-6,000	18.5	6.9	49.1	40.9	32.7
$6,000-8,000	} 5.8	.1	24.2	41.8	49.6
$8,000-10,000		—	2.3	10.5	6.8
Over $10,000	0.3	—	0.2	1.5	1.4

Distribution of Benefits Minus Distribution of all Families (per cent)

Annual Income	Public Housing[a]	Rent Supplements[b]	Rental Assistance[c]	Home Ownership[d]	Rural Housing[b]
Under $2,000	25.0	} 78.5	} 10.2	} −7.9	} −3.9
$2,000-4,000	29.7				
$4,000-6,000	3.1	−4.4	38.0	29.8	21.4
$6,000-8,000	} −28.1	−13.7	11.9	30.1	35.9
$8,000-10,000		} −60.3	−11.3	−1.8	−7.6
Over $10,000	−29.8		−48.9	−50.2	−45.5

a 1966   b 1969   c 1970   d 1971 1stQ

Table 5: Revenue Cost of Allowing Homeowners Deductions for Mortgage Interest and Real Estate Taxes, 1971

Adjusted Gross Income	Number of Returns		Deductions		Distribution of Tax Saving Relative to Distribution of Taxpayers 4.÷2.
	(thousands)	Per Cent of Total	Total Cost in millions of dollars	Per Cent of Total Cost	
	1.	2.	3.	4.	5.
Under $3,000	656	2.4	19.6	0.4	.17
$3,000-4,999	1,889	7.0	111.7	2.4	.34
$5,000-6,999	2,322	8.6	118.2	2.5	.29
$7,000-9,999	5,075	18.8	470.8	10.1	.53
$10,000-14,999	8,781	32.5	1,137.1	24.4	.74
$15,000-19,999	4,614	17.1	944.0	20.3	1.17
$20,000-49,999	3,295	12.2	1,355.7	29.1	2.35
$50,000-99,999	342	1.3	332.4	7.1	5.37
$100,000 and Over	87	0.3	163.9	3.5	11.65
TOTAL	27,060	100.0	4,653.1	100.0	—

Appendix B

Table B-1: Net Borrowing in Credit Markets, 1955-1980

Total funds borrowed in credit markets by nonfinancial sectors, excluding corporate equities (in billions of dollars)	Annual Averages			
	1955-59	1961-65	1966-70	1980
	$35.9	$58.2	$84.4	$161.7
A. AS PER CENT OF GNP:				
1. Total funds raised	8.2%	9.7%	9.8%	8.5%
2. U.S. Government[1]	.3	.9	.9	.2
3. Other	7.9	8.8	8.9	8.2
4. Municipals	1.1	1.0	1.0	1.2
5. Corporate and foreign bonds	1.1	.9	1.7	1.1
6. Housing mortgages	2.7	2.9	2.0	2.6
7. Other mortgages and loans	3.0	4.0	4.1	3.3
8. Sector totals	7.9	8.8	8.9	8.2
9. State and local governments[2]	1.2	1.0	1.1	1.3
10. Households	3.7	3.9	3.0	3.0
11. Nonfinancial business	2.7	3.3	4.5	3.9
12. Foreign	.3	.5	.3	.0
13. Memo: corporate equities not included above	.5	.2	.3	.6
B. AS PER CENT OF TOTAL FUNDS BORROWED:				
1. Total funds borrowed:	100.0%	100.0%	100.0%	100.0%
2. U.S. Government[1]	3.6	9.5	9.4	2.8
3. Other	96.4	90.5	90.6	97.2
4. Municipals	13.9	10.2	10.3	13.8
5. Corporate and foreign bonds	13.0	9.0	17.7	13.5
6. Housing mortgages	33.1	29.9	20.5	30.7
7. Other mortgages and loans	36.3	41.3	42.1	39.1
8. Sector totals	96.4	90.5	90.6	97.2
9. State and local governments[2]	14.2	10.7	10.8	15.0
10. Households	45.6	40.2	30.4	35.3
11. Nonfinancial business	33.3	34.2	45.9	46.3
12. Foreign	3.2	5.4	3.5	.6
13. Memo: corporate equities not included above	6.6	1.9	3.2	7.3

1/ Includes budget agency issues but excludes issues by federally sponsored credit agencies that are not included in the budget.

2/ Includes loans from U.S. Government.

Source: Stephen P. Taylor, "Long-Term Prospects for Housing Finance—A Projection to 1980," *Federal Reserve Staff Study: Ways to Moderate Fluctuations in Housing Construction* (Washington, D.C.: Board of Governors of the Federal Reserve System, December 1972).

Table B-2: Residential Mortgage Markets, 1955-1980[1]

	Annual Averages			
A. NET FLOWS OF CREDIT, PER CENT OF GNP:	1955-59	1961-65	1966-70	1980
1. Net funds raised	2.70%	2.90%	2.01%	2.60%
2. *Home mortgages*	2.47	2.34	1.53	1.75
3. *Multifamily*	.23	.56	.48	.85
4. Net funds advanced	2.70	2.90	2.01	2.60
5. *U.S. Government and sponsored agencies[2]*	.20	—.02	.40	.31
6. *Commercial banks*	.28	.39	.32	.48
7. *Savings institutions*	1.59	2.00	1.06	1.40
8. *Insurance and pension funds*	.47	.46	.19	.36
9. *Others*	.16	.07	.04	.05
10. Memo: FHLB advances[3]	.06	.14	.10	.08

	1954	1959	1965	1970	1980
B. BALANCES OUTSTANDING:					
1. Billions of dollars	$88	$148	$246	$333	$737
2. Per cent of GNP	24.1%	30.5%	35.9%	34.0%	38.6%
3. *Home mortgages*	20.5	26.6	30.5	28.2	29.1
4. *Multifamily*	3.7	3.9	5.4	5.9	9.5
Distribution of outstandings, by holder					
5. Home mortgages	100.0%	100.0%	100.0%	100.0%	100.0%
6. *U.S. Government and sponsored agencies[2]*	3.7	4.2	3.1	7.4	10.0
7. *Commercial banks*	17.6	14.9	14.4	15.2	18.8
8. *Savings institutions*	45.6	51.9	59.8	59.4	59.6
9. *Insurance and pension funds*	20.6	19.1	15.8	11.2	5.2
10. *Others*	12.5	9.9	6.9	6.8	6.4
11. Multifamily residential mortgages	100.0%	100.0%	100.0%	100.0%	100.0%
12. *U.S. Government and sponsored agencies*	2.0	4.8	2.8	5.8	12.4
13. *Commercial banks*	6.3	6.0	5.3	5.7	7.2
14. *Savings institutions*	34.8	38.8	48.8	45.6	43.7
15. *Insurance and pension funds*	27.1	24.9	33.8	39.6	34.8
16. *Others*	29.8	25.4	9.2	3.4	7.9

1/Excludes loans in process at savings institutions and U.S. Government liabilities for home mortgages. These are netted against the respective sector holdings.
2/Includes mortgage pools backing GNMA-guaranteed securities.
3/Credit to savings institutions.

Source: Stephen P. Taylor, "Long-Term Prospects for Housing Finance—A Projection to 1980," *Federal Reserve Staff Study: Ways to Moderate Fluctuations in Housing Construction* (Washington, D.C.: Board of Governors of the Federal Reserve System, December 1972).

Table B-3: Actual Rent Payments as Per Cent of Income

Family Income in 1967	Median Monthly Payments (in dollars)		Payments as Per Cent of Income (at midpoint)	
	Rent	Mortgage	Rent	Mortgage
Under $3,000	60	50	48	40
$3,000-4,999	70	60	20	18
$5,000-7,499	70	80	13	15
$7,500-9,999	90	90	12	12
$10,000-14,999	100	100	10	10
$15,000 and Over	140	130	less than 10	less than 10

Source: 1968 Survey of Consumer Finances conducted by the Survey Research Center, The University of Michigan.

Table B-4: Alternative Computation of Housing Poverty

Per Cent of Income Absorbed by Rent	Income Implied by Rent of $928	Households Receiving Implied Income or Less in 1971	
		Number (in millions)	Per Cent of All Households
40	$2,321	7.7	11.6
35	2,652	8.7	13.0
30	3,094	10.4	15.6
25	3,713	12.9	19.3

Sources: U.S. Bureau of Labor Statistics, *Monthly Labor Review* (April 1969), pp. 3-16, (June 1972), pp. 46-50; and U.S. Bureau of the Census *Current Population Reports,* Series p-60, No. 83 (July 1972).

CED Board of Trustees

See pages 5 and 6 for list of Research and Policy
Committee and the Subcommittee members
who are responsible for the conclusions
in this particular study.

Honorary Trustees

PUBLICATION ORDER FORM

To order CED publications please indicate number in column entitled "# Copies Desired." Then mail this order form and check for total amount in envelope to Distribution Division, CED, 477 Madison Ave., New York 10022.

ORDER NUMBER   STATEMENTS ON NATIONAL POLICY (paperbound)   **# COPIES DESIRED**

50P .. FINANCING THE NATION'S HOUSING NEEDS $1.50   _____
Examines the financal obstacles that hinder fulfillment of the nation's housing requirements and sets forth recommendations to make the nation's housing markets more responsive to the needs of all sectors of society. The statement proposes measures to assure that the total amount of housing finance required in the 1970's will in fact be forthcoming.

49P .. BUILDING A NATIONAL HEALTH-CARE SYSTEM $1.75   _____
Sets forth a plan for the organization, management, and financing of a national health care system which would improve the delivery of health care services while extending insurance coverage to all Americans. Includes an extensive review of the current health care system.

48P .. A NEW TRADE POLICY TOWARD COMMUNIST COUNTRIES $1.50   _____
CED and its counterparts in Europe and Japan propose the creation of a new global economic organization to develop rules governing trade and commercial relations between East and West. In an individual statement, CED recommends a continued easing of U.S. trade and credit restrictions against communist countries, bringing them in line with U.S. policies toward other industrialized nations.

47P .. HIGH EMPLOYMENT WITHOUT INFLATION: A POSITIVE PROGRAM FOR ECONOMIC STABILIZATION $1.50   _____
Recommends a continued governmnetal role in wage-price policies, calls for basic structural changes in the economy, and urges an incentive system of decontrol. Emphasizes that fiscal and monetary policies must remain the key element of the nation's economic efforts.

46P .. REDUCING CRIME AND ASSURING JUSTICE $1.50   _____
An integrated examination of needed reforms in the entire system of criminal justice, including courts, prosecution, police, and corrections.

45P .. MILITARY MANPOWER AND NATIONAL SECURITY $1.00   _____
Focuses on several critical issues relating to military manpower. Recommends an annual review by Congress of the sources and uses of military personnel. This proposal is designed to increase the accountability of the Executive Branch to the public while preserving needed Presidential flexibility in dealing with emergencies.

44P .. THE UNITED STATES AND THE EUROPEAN COMMUNITY $1.50   _____
Deals with the development of the Common Market into an enlarged European Economic Community and its potential effects on Western European trade, investment, and monetary relations with the U.S. and other free-world nations. Recommends immediate steps to halt deterioration in the world trading system.

43P .. IMPROVING FEDERAL PROGRAM PERFORMANCE $1.50   _____
Focuses attention on three major areas of concern about federal programs: (1) the choice of policy goals and program objectives, (2) the selection of programs that will achieve those objectives, and (3) the execution of the programs and the evaluation of their performance.

42P .. SOCIAL RESPONSIBILITIES OF BUSINESS CORPORATIONS $1.50   _____
Develops a rationale for corporate involvement in solving such pressing social problems as urban blight, poverty, and pollution. Examines the need for the corporation to make its social responsibilities an integral part of its business objectives. Points out at the same time the proper limitations on such activities.

41P .. EDUCATION FOR THE URBAN DISADVANTAGED: From Preschool to Employment $1.50   _____
A comprehensive review of the current state of education for disadvantaged minorities; sets forth philosophical and operational principles which are imperative if the mission of the urban schools is to be accomplished successfully.

40P .. FURTHER WEAPONS AGAINST INFLATION $1.50   _____
Examines the problem of reconciling high employment and price stability. Maintains that measures to supplement general fiscal and monetary policies will be needed—including the use of voluntary wage-price (or "incomes") policies, as well as measures to change the structural and institutional environment in which demand policy operates.

39P .. MAKING CONGRESS MORE EFFECTIVE $1.00   _____
Points out the structural and procedural handicaps limiting the ability of Congress to respond to the nation's needs. Proposes a far-reaching Congressional reform program.

38P .. DEVELOPMENT ASSISTANCE TO SOUTHEAST ASIA $1.50   _____
Deals with the importance of external resources—financial, managerial, and technological, including public and private—to the development of Southeast Asia.

37P .. TRAINING AND JOBS FOR THE URBAN POOR $1.25   _____
Explores ways of abating poverty that arises from low wages and chronic unemployment or underemployment. Evaluates current manpower training and employment efforts by government and business.

36P .. IMPROVING THE PUBLIC WELFARE SYSTEM $1.50   _____
Analyzes the national problem of poverty and the role played by the present welfare system. The statement recommends major changes in both the rationale and the administration of the public assistance program, with a view to establishing need as the sole criterion for coverage.

35P .. RESHAPING GOVERNMENT IN METROPOLITAN AREAS $1.00   _____
Recommends a two-level system of government for metropolitan areas: an area-wide level and a local level comprised of "community districts."

SEE OTHER SIDE—

34P . . ASSISTING DEVELOPMENT IN LOW-INCOME COUNTRIES $1.25   _____
        Offers a sound rationale for public support of the U.S. economic assistance program
        and recommends a far-ranging set of priorities for U.S. Government policy.

33P . . NONTARIFF DISTORTIONS OF TRADE $1.00   _____
        Examines the complex problem of dealing with nontariff distortions of trade arising
        from governmental measures that create special barriers to imports and incentives
        to exports.

32P . . FISCAL AND MONETARY POLICIES FOR STEADY ECONOMIC GROWTH $1.00   _____
        Reexamines the role of fiscal and monetary policies in achieving the basic economic
        objectives of high employment, price stability, economic growth, and equilibrium
        in the nation's international payments.

31P . . FINANCING A BETTER ELECTION SYSTEM $1.00   _____
        Urges comprehensive modernization of election and campaign procedures at
        national, state, and local levels. Proposes ways to reduce costs and spread them
        more widely through tax credits.

30P . . INNOVATION IN EDUCATION $1.00   _____
        Examines the problems of the American schools, reviews educational goals and
        opportunities (including technological resources), and explores relative costs and
        benefits. Sets forth comprehensive recommendations for change.

28P . . MODERNIZING STATE GOVERNMENT $1.00   _____
        Recommends sweeping renovation of state governments and their constitutions. Pro-
        poses granting legislatures broad powers to deal with problems of a rapidly-changing
        era; strengthening executive capability through modern management methods; im-
        proving the administration of justice; and furthering intergovernmental relations.

27P . . TRADE POLICY TOWARD LOW-INCOME COUNTRIES $1.50   _____

24P . . HOW LOW INCOME COUNTRIES CAN ADVANCE THEIR OWN GROWTH $1.50   _____

23P . . MODERNIZING LOCAL GOVERNMENT $1.00   _____

22P . . A BETTER BALANCE IN FEDERAL TAXES ON BUSINESS   75¢   _____

21P . . BUDGETING FOR NATIONAL OBJECTIVES $1.00   _____

15P . . EDUCATING TOMORROW'S MANAGERS $1.00   _____

14P . . IMPROVING EXECUTIVE MANAGEMENT IN THE FEDERAL GOVERNMENT $1.50   _____

9P . . ECONOMIC LITERACY FOR AMERICANS   75¢   _____

1P . . ECONOMIC GROWTH IN THE UNITED STATES $1.00   _____

Quantity discounts: 10-24 copies—10%, 25-49 copies—15%, 50-99 copies—20%, 100-249 copies—30

NOTE TO EDUCATORS: Instructors in colleges and universities may obtain
up to 5 free copies of those CED Statements on National Policy which they in-
tend to use in courses they are teaching. Please mention the course name when
ordering. For more than 5 copies, an educational discount of 20% will apply.
Course ....

☐ I am enclosing $................................ for the copies ordered above.

☐ Please bill me. *(Payment must accompany orders under $10.00)*

DO YOU WANT ALL CED PUBLICATIONS WHEN ISSUED?

☐ I would like to obtain all CED publications as soon as they are issued. Please send
me information about the CED Reader Forum subscription plan.

☐ Please send me newest list of publications.

Name ....

Organization ....

Address ....

City .... State .... Zip ....

      ☐ Businessman   ☐ Educator   ☐ Professional

✺CED International Library

Increasingly close relationships are being developed with independent, nonpolitical research organizations in other countries. These organizations are composed of businessmen and scholars, have objectives similar to those of CED, and pursue them by similarly objective methods. In several cases, agreements for reciprocal distribution of publications have developed out of this cooperation.

CEDA Committee for Economic Development of Australia
343 Little Collins Street, Melbourne, Victoria

CEPES Europäische Vereinigung für
Wirtschaftliche und Soziale Entwicklung
56 Friedrichstrasse, Dusseldorf, West Germany

PEP Political and Economic Planning
12 Upper Belgrave Street,
London, SWIX 8BB, England

経済同友会 Keizai Doyukai
(Japan Committee for Economic Development)
Japan Industrial Club Bldg.
1 Marunouchi, Chiyoda-ku, Tokyo, Japan

CED Council for Economic Development
Economic Development Foundation
P.O. Box 1896, Makati, Rizal, Philippines

CRC Centre de Recherches et d'Etudes des Chefs d'Entreprise
31 Avenue Pierre 1er de Serbie, Paris (16ème), France

SNS Studieförbundet Näringsliv och Samhälle
Sköldungagatan 2, 11427 Stockholm, Sweden

ESSCB Ekonomik ve Sosyal Etüdler Konferans Heyeti
279/8 Cumhuriyet Cad. Adli Han
Harbiye, Istanbul, Turkey

Committee for Economic Development